TARANT...
TARANTARA!

A Musical Play

IAN TAYLOR

SAMUEL   FRENCH

LONDON

NEW YORK   TORONTO   SYDNEY   HOLLYWOOD

TARANTARA! TARANTARA!

First presented by the Bristol Old Vic Company on May 20th, 1975. Subsequently presented at the Westminster Theatre, London, and the Phoenix Theatre, London, with the following cast of characters:

Joe, a stage hand	Jonathan Darvill
Richard D'Oyly Carte	George Raistrick
Jessie Bond	Judith Coke
Geraldine Ulmar	Hazel McBride
Sybil Grey	Sue Withers
Sir Arthur Sullivan	Timothy Kightley
George Grossmith	Mark Buffery
W. S. Gilbert	Christopher Scoular
Stage Hands	Roger Farrent, Julia Chambers, David Finlayson

The Play directed by David Horlock
Setting by John McMurray

The play opens Back-stage at the Savoy Theatre on October 3rd, 1888

CASTING

This piece is meant to be performed in the spirit of pantomime, in fact it would suit this kind of entertainment very well. Also, so long as the text is not interfered with, more actors, or a bigger chorus could be used. Therefore, in the case of a large company some people could be there just to sing.

SETTING

Permanently on stage are the following: **Gilbert**'s desk, with chair or stool, and an umbrella stand; on the opposite side, **Sullivan**'s podium, with music-stand and padded seat, and a hat-stand, table and chair nearby; up C, **Carte**'s table and chair. A piano and stool are set where convenient, or may be placed in the orchestra pit. One or two other bent-wood chairs as desired.

Furnishings and props for the excerpts from the various operas may be as simple or as elaborate as facilities allow, and are brought on or struck by the three stage hands, at the appropriate moments.

MUSICAL NUMBERS

The "characters" in the operatic excerpts are played and sung by members of the cast: the allocations are indicated at the appropriate points in the text. The same procedure is followed when the cast play other characters (e.g. Geraldine Ulmar as Helen Lenoir, see p. 15).

FURNITURE AND PROPERTIES

All that is strictly necessary for the operatic excerpts is a suggestion (more or less elaborate as desired) of the characters represented—e.g. a wig for the **Judge** in Trial by Jury (see p. 11), a hat and jacket for **Carte** and **Gilbert** to exchange in *H.M.S. Pinafore* (see p. 26), etc.

ACT I

A MUSIC REHEARSAL FOR *THE YEOMEN OF THE GUARD*

The Pianist is playing, and Joe, a Stage Hand, is sweeping the floor of the stage and whistling the music. Carte enters and goes up to him

Joe (*cheerfully*) Hello, Mr Carte.
Carte Hello, Joe. Got this one, then?
Joe Yes, Mr Carte. I know 'em all. I'm everyone's understudy.
Carte Everybody in to rehearsal today?

The actresses enter—Jessie Bond, Geraldine Ulmar, and Sybil Grey. They say "Hello" to Carte, who sits on the edge of his desk. They take off their outdoor clothes and hand them to the Stage Hands, who take them off stage

Jessie Bond goes across to the Pianist

Jessie Mr White, can you hear my first song before Sir Arthur arrives?

The Pianist plays the intro. Carte sits at his desk and works. Jessie sings a few lines of "When a Maiden Loves" and then fluffs. She stops and swears under her breath

> When maiden loves, she sits and sighs,
>   She wanders to and fro
> Unbidden tear-drops fill her eyes,
> And to all questions she replies
>   With a sad "heigh-ho!"

Oh Gawd, I've gone and forgotten the words and I knew them this morning. Can I try it again, Mr White? I've got to get this thing right. The curtains open and there's me sitting there at the spinning-wheel. (*A broad hint at Carte*) I can't think why they didn't use a chorus to open the show as they always do?

The Pianist plays again. Jessie reads her script

Sullivan enters, with rolls of music under his arm

The Pianist stops playing

Sullivan Good afternoon, ladies and gentlemen.
All Good afternoon, Sir Arthur.

Sullivan Hello, Carte.

Carte nods and smiles, then continues working. Joe looks at his watch, then helps Sullivan take off his coat, which he hangs on the stand

    (*As he is helped off with his coat*) I am frightfully sorry if I've delayed everybody. I know we must make the most of these music rehearsals. (*A broad hint at Carte*) They are so few and time's precious. Thank you, Mr White. Is George Grossmith here?

Joe George! You're wanted!

Grossmith enters nervously. He holds up a music sheet, shaking his head

Grossmith I'll never get this one. (*He stops on seeing Carte*)

Sullivan (*giving him another sheet of music*) We'll have a go at that one later. The one I'm worried about is your buffoon song. That is going to give us a lot of trouble. I'd like to go through it with you before Mr Gilbert arrives.

All Ugh!

Grossmith Oh. He is not coming in today?

Sybil He's brought things grinding to a halt twice this week.

Geraldine Can't you keep him out, Mr Carte?

Jessie Well, I'm ready for him this time, if he starts anything.

Sullivan (*almost sarcastically*) There are one or two songs he's worried about.

Grossmith That makes two of us.

Sullivan Three of us. I still haven't been able to set the one with the Heighdy Chorus.

Grossmith "I have a song to sing O." That one?

Sullivan Yes. I have a song to set o—and I don't know how I'm going to do it.

Carte laughs—and waves as if to say "You'll do it, Arthur"

    No really, it doesn't make any musical sense. (*He looks about to indulge in complaints about Gilbert's words then stops*)

Grossmith (*very worriedly*) But I will have it in time to learn it? I mean, I won't have the song just as I'm about to step on the stage like . . .?

Sullivan (*with charm*) Yes, yes, George, you shall have it in plenty of time. You shall have the song even if I have to get Mr Gilbert to set it himself.

Carte laughs. Sullivan laughs with him

Geraldine Heaven forbid. Sir Arthur.

Gilbert Yes, Miss Ulmar.

Geraldine Will you hear the song I sing with Fairfax?

Jessie And mine.

Sybil And mine.

Sullivan Yes. Yes. I must hear all the songs I've set so far whilst I have the chance. But I'll hear George first. So when you are ready, George.

After some preparations, Grossmith sings the first verse—"Oh a private buffoon is a light-hearted loon" (Refer to the music score for verse)

Yes, well, it'll be there, George, it'll be there. But I do prefer my tune! Let's try the last verse, shall we?

Grossmith sings the last verse—"Though your head it may rack" (For words, refer to the music score, fifth verse)

During the singing of this verse Gilbert enters hobbling. He is very bad tempered

Grossmith (*singing*) . . . "They don't blame you so long as you're funny."
Gilbert (*giving a roar of sarcastic laughter*) Funny? Funny eh, Grossmith? Funny? It would be funny if we could hear the words. The words are funny. Bloody funny. If they're not garbled. And you are garbling, Grossmith. Garbling. I suppose this play will be like all the others before it, we'll hear *Sir* Arthur's music all right. Everybody will go into raptures over Sir Arthur's music, but of my words not a whit will be heard. Not a bloody whit. Now you've made me swear, Grossmith, and I don't like swearing when ladies are present.
Jessie Oh, don't mind us, Mr Gilbert.
Actresses No, don't mind us . . .

Joe helps Gilbert off with his coat

Gilbert I'm not minding you. There are cleaning ladies in the building . . .
Jessie Oh, dear . . .

In turning away from Joe, Gilbert bumps into the Actresses

Gilbert Kindly get out of the way and let me get to my desk. You're holding up my work . . .

Joe hangs up Gilbert's coat

Jessie Don't you speak to me like that!
Sybil We're not chorus girls, you know!
Gilbert Oh! Aren't you? Who took you out of the back row of the chorus? And I can put you back whenever I like.
Jessie (*aside*) Oh my Gawd. I'm going to ask for more money.
Gilbert (*overhearing the remark*) You'll not get it. We'll have no stars here, Jessie Bond . . .

Gilbert shuffles across to his desk. He glares at Carte as acknowledgement and settles at his desk. Jessie protests

Sullivan (*who has been studiously ignoring Gilbert; to Grossmith*) Thank you, George. Oh, Jessie, Jessie, Jessie, if you come over here, please, I'll go through that opening song with you line by line until we get the rhythm of it.
Gilbert (*from behind his desk*) Wait a minute! Let me get up to the back

there! If Jessie Bond is going to warble I want to be able to hear right up there, every word. Every syllable.

Sullivan (*suddenly breaking*) Mr Gilbert! This is a music rehearsal.

Gilbert I am aware of that, sir!

Sullivan And I am in charge of it.

Gilbert You, sir, are in charge of the crochets, minims and quavers and all those other absurd characters. *I* am in charge of the *words*—the action—and everything else . . .

Sullivan But you have no right to be here today, sir.

Gilbert I've as much right as you, sir.

Sullivan Only with *my* permission! Music rehearsal days are *my* days.

Carte Yes, come on, Gilbert, old man, settle down.

Gilbert Oh! I know you and Sullivan would like me to stay away altogether.

Sullivan (*appealing to Carte*) This is ridiculous. I'm trying to help these people to sing.

Gilbert I'm surprised to find you here at all. I'm surprised that you were able to tear yourself away from your social engagements.

Sullivan My private life has nothing to do with you, sir.

Gilbert It has when it interferes with *my* plays.

Sullivan Your plays. What do you mean?

Gilbert It's no wonder you're always ill. The way you live.

Sullivan That is my affair.

Gilbert You make me ill.

Sullivan I repeat. Nothing to do with you.

Gilbert Well, there's one good thing for you, Sullivan, you have plenty of lady admirers to give you sympathy.

Whilst Sullivan looks about to explode—Gilbert adds under his breath

No wonder you're always ill. Vicious circle, if you ask me.

Sullivan Carte! This man has completely destroyed the whole atmosphere for rehearsal. We cannot go on.

Gilbert You don't need much of an excuse to give up work, do you?

Carte (*rising and coming down*) This isn't playing the game you know, Gilbert.

Gilbert You keep out of it and do your sums—money is your game, Carte! Confine your thoughts to money.

Carte How dare you!

Sullivan Oh, this is impossible. Get me my coat!

Gilbert Stay here and earn *your* money.

Sullivan You—don't need me! You don't need a musician. What you need is a barrel organ . . .

Gilbert Yes—I've already got the monkey.

Sullivan (*beside himself with temper, hopping on the spot*) What did you say, sir?

Carte I give up! (*He goes to his desk*)

Sullivan (*pointing across Carte at Gilbert*) Let me tell you, sir. I am entitled to some respect from *you*!

Gilbert I'll give you respect when you behave worthily of respect.   4

*Both men glare at each other. Joe whistles. Gilbert, Sullivan and Carte
freeze*
Piano—"Lord High Executioner"

Joe On my right . . .

GILBERT BEFORE SULLIVAN. SULLIVAN BEFORE GILBERT

. . . Gilbert. Born eighteenth November eighteen thirty-six, seventeen
Southampton Street, Strand. His grandfather's house . . .
Jessie His grandfather knew Dr Johnson, Garrick and Reynolds. He is
said to be descended from Sir Humphrey Gilbert.
Sybil He is christened William . . .
Jessie Schwenck—Gilbert.
Grossmith At the age of two, while on holiday in Italy, he is stolen from
his nurse by brigands and taken to the mountains.
Jessie Pity he didn't stay there.
Geraldine But he is ransomed.
Jessie For twenty-five pounds.   4a
Joe On my left, six years later. Sullivan—born eight Bolwell Terrace.

Piano

Gilbert Lambeth. The unfashionable side of the river.
Joe Please! Thirteenth May eighteen forty-two.   4b
Sullivan The year of Mendelssohn's *Spring Song*.
Grossmith Sullivan makes discoveries for himself on the parlour piano.
Jessie And he's only eight.
Grossmith He is christened Arthur . . .
Sullivan Seymour Sullivan.
Gilbert Initials, A.S.S.
Geraldine Father—Irish. Clarinet player.
Gilbert Mother looks after an organ grinder's monkey.   4c
All Shshsh!
Joe Sullivan's father is bandmaster at Sandhurst.

Piano

Geraldine He lets him play all the instruments in the band.
Sybil He composes his first anthem.   4d
Jessie And he's only eight.
Gilbert Aah . . .
Joe Gilbert at Great Ealing School.
Grossmith (*as Schoolmaster*) If Gilbert took more pains with his lessons,
and less in fighting and writing plays, he might do well . . .   4e
Jessie Sullivan is educated . . .
Sullivan Privately.
Geraldine In Bayswater.
Grossmith Dear Mrs Sullivan . . .
Joe The Reverend Thomas Helmore.
Geraldine Principal of the *Chapel Royal*!

Grossmith (*as Helmore*) Dear Mrs Sullivan, Arthur sang a very elaborate solo in church today. His expression brought tears to my eyes, but as I was immediately to enter the pulpit, I restrained myself.

Jessie Bless his little heart.

Sullivan Dear Mother, the Prince Consort heard me sing, and gave me half a guinea . . .

Gilbert Tip the monkey, ladies and gentlemen, and he'll turn the handle!   **4f**

Gilbert at university

Why do I have to study Shakespeare? I have nothing to learn from him. He's all gibberish. For instance, what does this mean? "I would as lief be thrust through a thicket hedge as cry pooh to a callow throstle."

Grossmith (*as Tutor*) Obvious, obvious. A great lover of songsters rather than disturb a little warbler would prefer to go through a thorny hedge. But I cannot place the quotation.

Gilbert I've just made it up.   **4g**

Fanfare

Joe Eighteen fifty-six: Sullivan wins Mendelssohn Scholarship to the Royal Academy of Music.

Jessie And he's only seventeen.

Joe Gilbert's first success as a writer.

Gilbert *The Laughing Song*. A translation by . . .

Fanfare

Joe Sullivan wins the chance to study at the Leipzig Conservatoire.   **4h**

Jessie The ladies flock to him.

Sybil (*as Student*) Oh, I am so impressed with Arthur. He is a natural courtier. When my turn comes to play I have no thoughts for anyone only how to impress this curly haired youth . . .

Sullivan Dear Mother and Father, it's such fun conducting here at the Conservatoire. I can fancy Mother saying, "Bless his little heart. How it must be beating."

Gilbert Bless his little heart.   **4j**

Joe Gilbert tries to join the army.

Gilbert I want a commission to go and fight in the Crimean War.

Grossmith (*as Army Officer*) The Crimean War's over, sonny.

Gilbert Oh—well in that case . . .

Joe Gilbert joins the Civil Service.

Gilbert The worst bargain the Government ever made.

Joe Gilbert receives a legacy of three hundred pounds.

Gilbert Escapes from the Civil Service . . .

Joe And becomes a Barrister at Law . . .

Gilbert My lords . . .

Joe In four years he earns—twenty-five pounds.

Sullivan sits on the podium stool

Gilbert The other night from cares exempt
       I slept and what do you think I dreamt?
       I dreamt that somehow I had come   **4k**
       To dwell in Topsy Turveydom.
Joe Gilbert writes the *Bab Ballads*!

The Company, except for Sullivan, gather round Gilbert

Grossmith The Editor of *Fun* requests Mr Gilbert to contribute one
column of copy per week for the rest of his natural life.
Gilbert I've jibe and joke
       And quip and crank
       For lowly folk
       And men of rank.
       I ply my craft
       And know no fear
       But aim my shaft
       At Prince or Peer
       At Peer or Prince—at Prince or Peer
       I aim my shaft and know no fear!
       I've wisdom from the East and from the West
       That's subject to no academic rule
       You may find it in the jeering of a jest
       Or distil it from the folly of a fool.
       I can teach you with a quip if I've a mind
       I can trick you into learning with a laugh;
       Oh winnow all my folly folly folly and you'll find
       A grain or two of truth among the chaff.
       Oh winnow all my folly folly folly and you'll find
       A grain or two of truth among the chaff.

Gilbert sits at his desk

Joe Sullivan soars to even greater success.

The Company move away to Sullivan

Jessie Have you heard his *Tempest* at the Crystal Palace?
Grossmith Magnificent. The audience went wild.
Jessie I always go along to St Michael's to hear him play the organ; don't
you?
Grossmith No, but I have heard that Birmingham have asked him to
compose something for their next festival.
Sullivan (*rising*) I feel like a missionary spreading the light of music to
those dark satanic cities of the north.
Jessie Did you hear he has composed a wedding march specially for
Princess Alexandra?
Sybil And a special song—*Bride of the North*.
Geraldine I have just heard Sullivan's Cello Concerto—splendid.
Jessie Ah, but you should hear his Symphony in E, my dear, out of this
world.

Geraldine A new master of English music.

Jessie The first musician of our time.

Sullivan There is so much to do for music if God would give me two days
for every one in which to do it.   4l

Gilbert (*rising*) Excuse me!

All turn to Gilbert

Joe Gilbert sells his first play to Tom Robertson, the famous director.

Gilbert Dulcimara or the little duck and the great quack; written in ten
days—containing dances, sketches, mysteries, love potions, warriors, and
lovesick maidens—a grand allegorical tableau of love's devices.

Grossmith (*as Robertson*) Hmmm, yes, this'll do. Thirty pounds.

Gilbert Pounds. I don't deal in pounds. Make it guineas.

Grossmith We don't deal in guineas.

Gilbert Very well. Thank you, sir.

Grossmith Here.

Gilbert Yes.

Grossmith Before you go, take a little bit of advice from an old stager.
Never sell as good a piece as this for thirty pounds ever again.   4n

Joe From now on Gilbert has no time for the high and mighty.

Grossmith Hey, you there.

Gilbert Me?

Grossmith Yes, you. Call me a cab.

Gilbert If you insist. You are a fourwheeler, sir.

Grossmith How dare you call me a fourwheeler!

Gilbert Well, I could hardly call you handsome.   4n

Joe Romance. Gilbert marries the daughter of an Indian Army officer.
Lucy Agnes . . .

Gilbert Kitten.

Joe Sullivan is pursued by Miss Rachel Scott Russell.

Sullivan moves off the podium

Jessie (*as Rachel*) Father built the Crystal Palace.

Joe She encourages him—to write music.

Jessie (*as Rachel, moving to Sullivan*) Dear, Arthur, how is your Symphony in D? Do write it. It is the language you speak to me.

Sullivan Yes, Rachel.

Jessie And dearest, I want you to write an opera—a grand, vigorous
work.

Sullivan Yes, Rachel—when I come back from Paris. By the by, what do
you want from Paris?

Jessie Three pairs of cool cotton stockings. Blue is my favourite colour—
and darling . . .

Sullivan Yes, dearest?

Jessie I want you to write an octet—grander than Mendelssohn. Say you'll
do it for me. Oh dearest, what will you do next?

Grossmith I say, Sullivan.

Jessie moves away

Joe Frederick Burnand, future editor of *Punch*.
Gilbert And minor playwright.
Grossmith (*as Burnand*) Will you do me a personal favour?
Sullivan Of course, old chap, if I can.
Grossmith Good. Well, you couldn't knock together a bit of music for some private entertainment. No money, I'm afraid. Might be fun though.
Sullivan What is it?
Grossmith Well, it's a sort of burlesque operetta.
Sullivan Oh?
Grossmith Just for a bit of fun.
Sullivan It might be rather a lark. What are you going to call it? **4o**
Grossmith It's from *Box and Cox*. I thought we'd call it *Cox and Box*.
Sullivan Give me a few days. Tell me the story.
Grossmith It's about these two chaps who share the same room without knowing it. Their landlord is a military man.

Light change—taped applause

I say, Sullivan. They're putting on *Cox and Box* at the Adelphi. It's a huge success. We must do another one.
Geraldine What is Sullivan thinking about squandering his genius in burlesque operetta?
Sybil I thought he was supposed to be a serious composer.
Jessie Arthur, write me an oratorio.
Sullivan I'm trying to get down to my oratorio.
Grossmith But they want to commission another burlesque operetta.
Sullivan But there's this oratorio of mine.
Grossmith But there's money in this one.
Sullivan Have you an idea?
Grossmith Yes. I'm going to call it *The Contrabandista*, an adventure in the Spanish Mountains.
Sullivan *The Contrabandista*.

Piano chord

Joe The box office takings do not cover the cost of the orchestra—and **4p** Sullivan returns to his oratorio.
Jessie I'm far prouder of the *Prodigal Son* than of anything. Everyone here is talking of your success.
Sullivan So are all my friends. The Empress Eugenie, the Tzar and Tzarina of Russia. The Prince of Wales.
Jessie The *Prodigal Son* has made you the man of the hour.
Sullivan I have had a letter from Queen Victoria.
Sybil (*as Queen Victoria*) Dear Mr Sullivan. We wish to receive a complete set of all your works—and we wish you to cast a critical eye over the compositions of our dear consort.
Joe And now——

Fanfare

—the first meeting. **4q**

All move away except Gilbert and Sullivan. Carte sits at his desk

Sullivan Mr Gilbert, I'm so pleased to meet you. I've heard so much about your work. In fact I do believe I have seen one of your plays. Ummm—*Robert the Devil*—it was very good, very good.

Gilbert Very good, was it?

Sullivan Yes, very good—very ummm—good.

Gilbert Of course this is the point where I am supposed to say that one hears your music wherever one goes.

Sullivan Oh, you are a lover of music?

Gilbert I only know two tunes—one is "God Save The Queen", the other is "Pop goes the Weasel". Neither of them is yours, is it?

Sullivan No. No.

Gilbert Mmm—pity, thought one of them might have been. Still Sullivan since you are here perhaps you would consider . . .   **4r**

Fanfare. The Company draw round again. Joe holds up a poster "Thespis"

Geraldine We don't think much of that.

Sybil It's not what we're used to.

Jessie We expected pantomime, not a long, boring tale about a lot of seedy gods.

Carte (*rising*) It runs for only sixty-seven performances. (*He comes down*)   **4s**

Fanfare

    Richard D'Oyly Carte.

Geraldine Art lover.

Grossmith Gourmet.

Sybil Impresario.

Carte Now manager of the Royalty, Soho.

Jessie Some people call him Oily Carte.

Joe He has a genius for backing outsiders.

Sullivan sits on the podium

CARTE AND *TRIAL BY JURY*

Carte Mr Gilbert. Carte.

Gilbert Oh, yes?

Carte Very fortunate meeting you like this.

Gilbert Fortunate for whom?

Carte For both of us, I trust.

Gilbert Oh?

Carte Yes, I—er—find myself in a bit of a predicament. I'm producing some entertainment at the Royalty in March, only a couple of weeks or so away—Offenbach's *La Perichole* . . .

Gilbert Offenbach again?

Carte shrugs and smiles

Carte Yes, I know, I know, exactly, Mr Gilbert. But even so, the pro-

gramme is too short. I need another one-act musical piece. I'd like it to
be a new one.

Gilbert There must be many around.

Carte But not written by Gilbert and Sullivan . . .

Gilbert Gilbert and . . . ?

Carte Sullivan.

Gilbert Oh. Him! Well. I doubt if he'd be interested in doing any more
work with me. He's too busy uplifting British music at present. They
say he's working for a knighthood. He does have the knack of slipping
a tune in the right quarter.

Carte Yes, but he is living beyond his means. He needs a lot of money to
keep up with his contacts and his racing, cards, roulette—you can't lead
that sort of life on the money you can earn for writing oratorio!

Gilbert Come to the point, Carte.

Carte (*directly*) I want a script from you. Have you one?

Gilbert I do happen to have one with me. (*Pulling out a tattered script*) It
is set in a court room.

Carte I was thinking of comic opera. Court rooms don't immediately
suggest themselves as comic opera.

Gilbert You've obviously never been in one of my courts . . .

Carte Come into my office. I'll get hold of Sullivan and you can read it to
him.

*Carte sits at his table. Gilbert and Sullivan take a chair each and sit either
side of it*

Gilbert (*bad-temperedly*) *Trial by Jury*, a dramatic cantata in one act.

Carte (*smiling, nodding as if already counting the audience*) Very nice.

Gilbert Scene. A court of justice. Barristers. Attorneys. Chorus . . .
Hark the hour of ten is sounding
Hearts with anxious fears are bounding
Hall of justice crowds surrounding
Breathing hope and fear . . .

5

Piano—"Hark the Hour of Ten is Sounding". Mime reading. Sullivan laughs

Sir, this farce is clearly beneath both of us. Sir, unless you stop laughing
and pay attention while I read, I must ask you to go outside. Sir, you
may think this is amusing.

Sullivan I do. I do. It's priceless. I can hear the tunes already.

Carte Then you'll do it?

Sullivan Of course I'll do it. How long may I have?

Carte We can't rush matters of this nature. Shall we say a fortnight?

Sullivan You shall have it in one week.

Carte Then, gentlemen—(*shaking hands with both of them*)—till we meet
again—in court.

*Music starts. The Company assemble. The Stage Hands set the Court unit
"Trial by Jury" sequence:*

TRIAL BY JURY

Judge (Gilbert) When I, good friends, was called to the bar,
    I'd an appetite fresh and hearty,
  But I was, as many young barristers are,
    An impecunious party.
  But I soon got tired of third-class journeys,
    And dinners of bread and water;
  So I fell in love with a rich attorney's
    Elderly, ugly daughter.
Chorus So he fell in love, etc.
Judge The rich attorney, he jumped with joy,
    And replied to my fond professions:
  "You shall reap the reward of your pluck, my boy
    At the Bailey and Middlesex Sessions.
  You'll soon get used to her looks," said he,
    "And a very nice girl you'll find her!
  She may very well pass for forty-three
    In the dusk, with a light behind her!"
Chorus She may very well, etc.

Gilbert polkas with Jessie

  In the dusk with a light behind her!

The Girls enter as a Chorus of Bridesmaids

  Comes the broken flower—
    Comes the cheated maid—
  Though the tempest lower,
    Rain and cloud will fade!
  Take, oh maid these posies:
    Though thy beauty rare
  Shame and blushing roses,
    They are passing fair!

(Repeat the last two lines)

  Wear the flowers till they fade;
  Happy be thy life, oh maid!

(Repeat the last line)

  Happy, happy, be thy life, oh maid.
Judge That she is reeling
    Is plain to see!
Foreman (Carte) If faint you're feeling
    Recline on me!

Jessie falls sobbing on to the Foreman's breast

Plaintiff (Sybil) *(feebly)* I shall recover
    If left alone.

All (*shaking their fists at Defendant*) Oh, perjured lover,
    Atone! Atone!
Foreman Just like a father
    I wish to be. (*Kissing her*)
Judge (*approaching her*) Or, if you'd rather,
    Recline on me!

Jessie jumps on to the Bench, sits down by the Judge, and falls sobbing on his breast

Counsel (Sullivan) Oh! Fetch some water
    From far Cologne!
All For this sad slaughter
    Atone! Atone!
Jury (*shaking their fists at the Defendant, all except Joe*)
    Monster, dread our fury . . .
    There's the Judge, and there's the Jury!
    Monster; monster, dread our fury!
Usher (Grossmith) Silence in court!
Judge Shhh.
Counsel Don't you worry about a thing, my dear.

SONG

Defendant (Joe) Oh gentlemen, listen, I pray,
    Though I own that my heart has been ranging;
Of nature the laws I obey,
    For nature is constantly changing.
The moon in her phases is found,
    The time and the wind and the weather,
The months in succession come round,
    And you don't find two Mondays together.
Consider the moral, I pray,

    Nor bring a young fellow to sorrow,
Who loves this young lady today,
    And loves that young lady tomorrow.
(*Repeat last four lines*)
Bridesmaids (*rushing forward, and kneeling to the Jury*)
    Consider the moral, etc.
All But this I am willing to say,
    If it will appease her sorrow,
I'll marry this lady today,
    And I'll marry the other tomorrow!

Chorus repeat brackets, changing

Plaintiff (*embracing him rapturously*)
    I love him—I love him—with fervour unceasing
    I worship and madly adore;

My blind adoration is ever increasing,
   My loss I shall ever deplore.
Oh, see what a blessing, what love and caressing
   I've lost, and remember it, pray,
When you I'm addressing, are busy assessing
   The damages Edwin must pay!
   Yes, he must pay!

Defendant (*repelling her furiously*)
   I smoke like a furnace—I'm always in liquor,
      A ruffian—a bully—a sot;
   I'm sure I should thrash her, perhaps I should kick her;
      I am such a very bad lot!
   I'm not prepossessing, as you may be guessing,
      She couldn't endure me a day;
   Recall my professing, when you are assessing
      The damages Edwin must pay!

Sybil clings to the Defendant passionately; after a struggle, he throws her off into the arms of Counsel

All Yes, he must pay.

RECITATIVE

Judge The question, gentlemen—is one of liquor;
     You ask for guidance—this is my reply:
     He says, when tipsy, he would thrash and kick her,
      Let's make him tipsy, gentlemen, and try!
Counsel With all respect
   I do object!
Plaintiff I do object!
Defendant I don't object!
All With all respect
   We do object!
   (*Refer to score for the Defendant*)
Judge (*tossing his books and papers about*)
   All the legal furies seize you!
   No proposal seems to please you,
   I can't sit up here all day,
   I must shortly get away.
   Barristers, and you, attorneys,
   Get you on your homeward journeys;
   Gentle, simple-minded Usher,
   Get you, if you like, to Rus*sher*;
   Put your briefs upon the shelf,
   I will marry her myself!

He comes down from the Bench to the floor of the court. He embraces Sybil

   For I am a judge.

All And a good judge too.
Judge Yes, I am a judge.
All And a good judge too!
Judge Though homeward as you trudge,
      You declare my law is fudge,
      Yet of beauty I'm a judge.
All And a good judge too!
Judge Though defendant is a snob...
Defendant No, no, no!
All And a great snob too! (*Repeat*)
      Though defendant is a snob
      And a great snob too
      He'll reward him from his fob
      So we've settled with the job.
      And a good job too.
   (*Refer to score for Judge*)

   After "Trial by Jury"

Applause. Gilbert and Sullivan return to their places. Gilbert sits at his desk, Sullivan stands at the podium, Carte stands at his table. The Stage Hands strike the Court unit

Carte I do believe we have a success overnight.
Helen (Geraldine) All London is whistling the tunes.
Joe Helen Lenoir, D'Oyly Carte's secretary, later his second wife.
Helen The popular critics are raving about the show.
Joe And Sullivan is dining out on his new-found success.

Joe goes off and returns with a tray of champagne glasses, which he hands out. The drinkers cluster round Sullivan

Jessie Do tell me, Arthur, are you happy?
Sullivan Am I happy? I don't know. I enjoyed the experience of putting on *Trial by Jury*, except for one slight altercation with Gilbert, who said at the end of one of the band rehearsals that he thought the music was "too loud"—tch—too loud!
Sir Alexander Cockburn (Grossmith) I liked your music, Sullivan...
Joe Sir Alexander Cockburn.
Jessie Lord Chief Justice.
Sullivan Thank you, sir.
Sir Alexander Cockburn I liked it very much indeed, but I don't like the *idea* of *Trial by Jury* at all—it is typical of that blasted Gilbert...
Sullivan I'm sorry to hear that...
Sir Alexander Cockburn It's all very clever and pretty, don't you know—but I shall never come and see it again, for fear of encouraging contempt of court—I'd get rid of that Gilbert if I were you!
Jessie I do agree, Sybil dear, don't you?

The drinkers retire. Carte moves down to Gilbert

Carte Er, Gilbert!

Gilbert (*at his desk, writing*) Mmm?

Carte What would you say to an English Comic Opera Company to oust the French?

Gilbert Sounds very grand. Where's the money coming from? I thought you were supposed to be reviving *Thespis*.

Carte The backers withdrew their money at the last moment.

Gilbert Surprising how these capitalists quail at the words "money down".

Carte The time is not right for *Thespis*. I want a new piece. A full-length opera.

Gilbert Don't ask me. I'm sticking to straight plays at the moment.

Carte Look, I'll raise the money. I'll form a company. With a board of directors. I've got my eye on a theatre in Wych Street.

Gilbert One—I want two hundred in advance . . .

Carte Pounds?

Gilbert Guineas.

Carte All right.

Gilbert Two—we choose our own company. Three, we control rehearsals. Four, we select the subject.

Carte I'll find Sullivan.

Joe But Sullivan has been frightened off by his critics.

"Musical Standard" Journalist (Geraldine) It is to be gathered from the public prints that the versatile composer of *Light of the World* has turned all his attention to musical burlesque.

Music Critic (Sybil) *Trial by Jury*, as far as Sullivan is concerned, is a joke, but it has gone far enough, and Sullivan will now turn his attention to the more serious subject of English opera.

Grossmith (*as Spokesman*) Lady Lindsay has taken Sullivan to recover in Italy.

Lady Lindsay (Jessie) A few weeks by Lake Como will inspire you to greater things than comic cantatas.

Carte I wish to speak to Mr Sullivan. Has he returned?

Grossmith (*shutting off Sullivan*) Mr Sullivan has returned from abroad.

Sybil But he has gone up to Cambridge.

Geraldine He is now Principal of the New National College of Music.

Jessie Dr Sullivan is so busy.

Sullivan (*writing*) "Dearest Mum, Princess Louise is coming to my party tomorrow—so bring lots of roses. Blow the expense. P.S. The guests will include the Prince of Wales, the Duchess of Westminster, the Lord Chief Justice . . . Mrs Ronalds . . ."

Sybil Dr Sullivan is there any truth in the rumour that you may marry Mrs Ronalds?

Sullivan laughs

Mrs Ronalds (Geraldine) Arthur Sullivan has kindly attended a few of my soirées—we are just—very good friends.

Carte Gilbert!
Gilbert I know, I know, Carte. (*Writing*) "Dear Sullivan, we are going to write a new opera. We'll call it *The Sorcerer*—it's about a modern magician who gives a whole village a love potion—with hilarious results. There is a wickedly funny part for your brother Fred—what do you say?"

6

Piano—"The Lost Chord"

Geraldine Dr Sullivan is not at home.
Grossmith Dr Sullivan is at the bedside of his dying brother.
Jessie Dr Sullivan's grief has inspired him to write *The Lost Chord.*
Sybil Dr Sullivan is in mourning for his brother.
Joe *The Lost Chord* is the most popular song in England.

The piano becomes livelier. Sybil, Jessie and Geraldine dance

Sullivan Please, I ask you, I wrote *The Lost Chord* in sorrow as my brother lay dying—don't burlesque it—besides, it affects the royalties. (*He sits*)

The piano finishes

The girls exit

Gilbert Dear Sullivan. Dear *Dr* Sullivan.
Sullivan Thank you.
Gilbert How are you getting on with the music for *The Sorcerer*? Can you help me to get the company together? Carte is badgering me.
Carte Gilbert, what is the delay with the new show?
Gilbert We are trying to find the right cast.
Carte Hurry up.
Gilbert You promised us full control.
Carte You already have that, but why aren't you moving faster?
Gilbert I want to form the basis, now, for a permanent company—no so-called stars—no temperamental tenors—they can't act and they are more trouble than the rest of the company put together. I'd rather take on a bunch of amateurs and lick them into shape.
Carte Just hurry up.
Sullivan Carte, Gilbert! Will you come down to Battersea. There's an entertainer there called Grossmith, ideal for our company, lecturing on Bombay.
Gilbert Bombay!
Carte Bombay!

Joe sets up a card table on which are a set of pictures for Grossmith's lecture

A poster:
George Grossmith Jnr entertains! New illuminated comic lecture: entitled "Bombay"

Grossmith Finally. It is very dark at night in the city of Bombay. This is my view of Bombay by night taken with my Kodachrome Viewfinder Master, purchased at Jidson's in the Strand . . . (*He holds up a completely black picture*) Details of any goods mentioned in the talk may be had on request. Oh, madam, madam—on your way out, you'll find that the manager of Jidson's has kindly set up a stall for your further interest in the lobby—there is so much to see in Bombay.

Gilbert (*approaching Grossmith*) Grossmith, Sullivan tells me that you were once in the hands of the law.

Joe strikes the card table

Grossmith I beg your pardon. Oh, yes. That's right. I was a police reporter —Bow Street.

Gilbert Miserable place—know it well. Now, I hear that Sullivan has auditioned you. We have just the part for you.

Grossmith But, Mr Gilbert, I'm not an opera singer. You need someone with a big strong voice for opera.

Gilbert That's just what we don't want. This is comic opera.

Grossmith Well, I never try to be funny—I mean: look funny—I don't make up. I never wear red noses . . .

Gilbert No red noses for us. We are not looking for clowns. Carte! Take him away. Sign him up.

Carte (*leading Grossmith over to his table*) I can offer you six pounds per week.

Grossmith Thank you.

Gilbert (*calling after Grossmith*) Grossmith, rehearsals start on Monday.

Grossmith signs the contract. Gilbert moves over to Sullivan

What's the matter, Sullivan? Your back bothering you again, you ought to go to bed at night instead of gadding around the clubs.

Sullivan I've been talking to Carte. He says the Board don't like us employing people like George . . .

Gilbert I know. But I want him.

Sullivan They want more professional entertainers . . .

Gilbert Bugger the Board!

Sullivan Pardon.

Gilbert Bugger 'em, Sullivan, bugger 'em.

Sullivan Er, quite.

Piano—"John Wellington Wells"

Gilbert We'll soon get George up to scratch. Get him started on *The Sorcerer*. You can work wonders on him.

Gilbert exits

Grossmith (*singing his best, at half speed*)
My name is John Wellington Wells,
I'm a dealer in magic and spells,
In blessings and curses . . .

He is stopped by Sullivan. The piano stops

Sullivan (*laughing*) No—no—George, George. No, no, not like that. You
see it says very *lively* . . .

The piano starts again

Grossmith I was being very lively . . .

Sullivan Yes, but it means even more very lively. I mean, it's a patter
song—goes like this . . .
(*Singing*) My name is John Wellington Wells.

THE SORCERER (SONG: Mr Wells)

Sullivan My name is John Wellington Wells,
    I'm a dealer in magic and spells,
       In blessings and curses
       And ever-filled purses,
    In prophecies, witches, and knells.

    If you want a proud foe to "make tracks"—
    If you'd melt a rich uncle in wax—
       You've but to look in
       On the resident Djinn,
    Number seventy, Simmery Axe!

Grossmith We've a first-rate assortment of magic;
       And for raising a posthumous shade
    With effects that are comic or tragic,
       There's no cheaper house in the trade
    Love-philtre—we've quantities of it;
       And for knowledge if any one burns,
    We keep a very small prophet, a prophet
       Who brings us unbounded returns:

    For he can prophesy
    With a wink *of* his eye,
    Peep with security
    Into futurity,
    Sum up your history,
    Clear up a mystery,
    Humour proclivity
    For a nativity—for a nativity;
    He has answers oracular
    Bogies spectacular
    Tetrapods tragical
    Mirrors so magical
    Facts astronomical,
    Solemn or comical,
    And, if you want it, he
    Makes a reduction on taking a quantity!

> Oh!
> If anyone anything lacks,
> He'll find it all ready in stacks,
>   If he'll only look in
>   On the resident Djinn,
> Number seventy, Simmery Axe!

Joe brings in a comic top hat and large bow. He puts the hat on Grossmith's head and gives the bow to Sullivan, who puts it around Grossmith's neck

Sullivan Put this round your neck, like that.
  Brighten you up a bit.

> He can raise you hosts
>   Of ghosts,
> **Grossmith** And that without reflectors;
> **Sullivan** And creepy things
>   With wings,
> **Grossmith** And gaunt and grisly spectres.
> **Sullivan** He can fill your crowds
>   Of shrouds,
> **Grossmith** And horrify you vastly;
> **Sullivan** He can rack your brains
>   With chains,
> **Grossmith** And gibberings grim and ghastly!
>   Then if you plan it, he

> Changes organity,
> With an urbanity,
> Full of Satanity,
> Vexes humanity
> With an inanity
> Fatal to vanity . . .

>   Driving your foes to the verge of insanity!

> Barring tautology,
> In demonology,
> 'Lectro-biology,
> Mystic nosology,
> Spirit philology,
> High-class astrology,
> Such is his knowledge, he;

>   Isn't the man to require an apology!

>   Oh!
> My name is John Wellington Wells,
> I'm a dealer in magic and spells,
>   In blessings and curses
>   And ever-filled purses,
> In prophecies, witches, and knells.

If anyone anything lacks,
He'll find it all ready in stacks,
    If he'll only look in
    On the resident Djinn,
Number seventy, Simmery Axe!

*Sullivan and Grossmith exit. Gilbert enters in a hurry and starts to cross the
stage*

Carte Ah, Gilbert. Where are you going to in such a hurry?

Gilbert I'm rushing this new plot to Sullivan.

Carte He's not there.

Gilbert Oh, not again.

Carte No. He's in Paris, recovering.

Gilbert It's all that high living. I suppose he's doing platonic tours of the
city at night with Mary Ronalds . . .

Carte No, I do believe he has been very ill, and down . . .

Gilbert Well, I'll post this off to him this might cheer him up.

Carte Before you do there is a slight problem.

Gilbert What? Out with it.

Carte It's my board of directors.

Gilbert Oh. Is it? I'm tired of that load of sharks. We've had nothing but
trouble with them. They wanted to take *The Sorcerer* off after the first
week.

Carte Box office takings were very low to begin with . . .

Gilbert Of course they were. It was something new. You have to be prepared to lose at first with something new. But the word went around,
and people started to come and see it. They soon changed their tune.
"Will you write us another opera?" Up one minute down the next.
Left to them they'd have killed us stone dead at the beginning. Now
what's wrong with them?

Carte They want to cut your advance.

Gilbert By how much?

Carte By half.

Gilbert The devil they do. Let me get my hands . . .

Carte I know. I know.

Gilbert And what did you say?

Carte Say?

Gilbert Say, yes, say.

Carte I did say it wouldn't do.

Gilbert You're damn right it won't do! Now look here, Carte. They
asked me to write a new book. Well, here it is. I stuck to my part of the
bargain, they must keep to theirs. They're damn lucky after *The Sorcerer*
I didn't ask for more money. Well, are you going to support me? If
not now is the time to tell me.

Sullivan enters

Carte Of course, of course, no question . . . Ah . . .

Gilbert (*to Sullivan*) Carte's right. You don't look well. I've got just the thing for you! Now, Carte, you go and deal with that pack of sharks. Sullivan and I are off to Portsmouth.

Carte exits

A whistle is heard off

GILBERT AND SULLIVAN AT PORTSMOUTH

Sullivan Portsmouth? Oh . . . yes . . .

Gilbert Salt sea air, Sullivan. This is it. You should get plenty of this down you. Did I tell you that the blood of Sir Humphrey Gilbert runs in my veins?

Sullivan (*smiling, with effort*) I believe you have mentioned it from time to time.

Joe enters as a sailor

Gilbert Ah, just look at the view, Sullivan. It's magnificent. I've never been so excited by an idea for a long time.

Gilbert stops a sailor (Joe)

Now tell me fine fellow, for you are a fine fellow . . .

Sailor (Joe) Yes, sir.

Gilbert Leading seaman, aren't you?

Sailor Yessir.

Gilbert I like the cut of your rig . . .

Sailor Thank you, sir.

Gilbert I think he'll do very well, don't you, Sullivan . . . ?

The sailor is dismissed. Joe exits

Piano—"H.M.S. Pinafore" music

I say, Sullivan, I've just had an idea . . . we'll have the uniforms made   8
here—make them really authentic, eh? And don't you like my idea about the First Sea Lord who has never been to sea? Could only happen in England that. It has got to have a truly English feel about it this play. The joke of English politics. The fact that we've made the First Sea Lord, Sir Joseph Porter, a radical of the most pronounced type, will allay any suspicions that it is W. H. Smith I'm getting at. They'll never guess. (*With his tongue in his cheek, behind Sullivan's back*) We don't want to upset anybody in high places, do we?

Sullivan splutters. Gilbert claps him on the back

This sea air does wonders. Of course, I'm not getting at anybody really. Just a bit of fun that's all. So long as we make it good and funny, we'll be forgiven, don't worry. Oh look, Sullivan, there's the *Victory*.

Sullivan Oh yes.

Gilbert Just imagine that on the back cloth—all the ropes and the rigging—Spithead in the distance—all the sailors waiting to welcome the First Sea Lord aboard. Can't you see it all growing before your eyes . . .

The Company enter for the "Pinafore" sequence

H.M.S. PINAFORE

Chorus (All) We sail the ocean blue,
    And our saucy ship's a beauty;
    We're sober men and true,
    And attentive to our duty.
    When the balls whistle free
    O'er the bright blue sea,
    We stand to our guns all day;
    When at anchor we ride
    On the Portsmouth tide,
    We have plenty of time for play.

    High
    Ahoy! Ahoy!
    Ahoy! Ahoy!
    Low

    The balls whistle free
    O'er the bright blue sea
All We stand to our guns to our guns all day
    We sail the ocean blue,
    And our saucy ship's a beauty.
    We're sober men and true
    And attentive to our duty.
    Our saucy ship's a beauty.
    We're attentive to our duty
    We're sober men and true
    We sail the ocean blue.

The Girls represent Sir Joseph's Female Relatives. They dance round the stage

Relatives (Girls) Gaily tripping,
    Lightly skipping,
    Flock the maidens to the shipping.
  (Repeat the last three lines)
Sailors (Men) Flags and guns and pennants dipping!
    All the ladies love the shipping.
Relatives Sailors sprightly
    Always rightly
    Welcome ladies so politely.

Sailors Ladies who can smile so brightly,
      Sailors welcome most politely.
   (*Repeat. Refer to score*)
      We're smart and sober men
      And quite devoid of fear
      In all the Royal N
      None are so smart as we are
Ladies Gaily tripping
      Lightly skipping
      Flock the maidens to the shipping.
   (*Repeat the last three lines*)
Sailors Sailors sprightly
      Always rightly.
      Welcome ladies so politely, so politely.
Ladies Gaily tripping
      Lightly skipping,
      Sailors always welcome ladies so politely.
   (*Repeat the last three lines*)
All (Counterpoint) Ladies who can smile so brightly
      Sailors welcome most politely, most politely.
      Gaily tripping
      Lightly skipping.
      Sailors always welcome ladies most politely.

Carte starts to sing immediately

Captain (Carte) Now give three cheers—
      I'll lead the way.
      Hip, hip, hip, hip—
All Hurray! Hurray!
      Hurray!

SONG

Sir Joseph (Sullivan) When I was a lad I served a term   9
      As office boy to an attorney's firm.
      I cleaned the windows and I swept the floor,
      And I polished up the handle of the big front door.
Chorus He polished up the handle of the big front door.
Sir Joseph I polished up that handle so carefullee
      That now I am the Ruler of the Queen's Navee!
Chorus He polished, etc.
Sir Joseph Now landsmen all, whoever you may be,
      If you want to rise to the top of the tree,
      If your soul isn't fettered to an office stool,
      Be careful to be guided by this golden rule—
Chorus Be careful, etc.
Sir Joseph Stick close to your desks and never go to sea
      And you all may be Rulers of the Queen's Navee!
Chorus Stick close, etc.

Gilbert Well, Carte. *Pinafore* seems to be very successful.
Carte Yes, ladies and gentlemen, owing to the success of *Pinafore* I've decided to take you up-river on a boat trip picnic.
All Cheers!

H.M.S. PINAFORE
RECITATIVE

Captain (*Carte*) My gallant crew, good morning.
All (*saluting*) Sir, good morning!
Captain I hope you're all quite well.
All (*as before*) Quite well; and you, sir?
Captain I am in reasonable health, and happy
    To meet you all once more.
All (*as before*) You do us proud, sir!

SONG

Captain I am the Captain of the *Pinafore*.
All And a right good captain, too!
Captain You're very, very good,
    And be it understood,
  I command a right good crew,
All We're very, very good
    And be it understood,
  He commands a right good crew.
Captain Though related to a peer,
    I can hand, reef, and steer
      Or ship a selvagee;
    I am never known to quail
    At the fury of a gale,
      And I'm never, never sick at sea!
All What, never?
Captain No, never!
All What, NEVER?
Captain Well—hardly ever!
All He's hardly ever sick at sea!
    Then give three cheers, and one cheer more
    For the hardy Captain of the *Pinafore*!
  (*Repeat the last two lines*)
Captain I do my best to satisfy you all—
All And with you we're quite content.
Captain You're exceedingly polite,
    And I think it only right
  To return the compliment.
All We're exceedingly polite,
    And he thinks it only right
  To return the compliment.

Captain Bad language or abuse
          I never, never use,
          Whatever the emergency;
          Though "BOTHER it" I may
          Occasionally say,
          I never use a big, big D—
All What, never?
Captain No, never!
All What, NEVER?
Captain Well, hardly ever!
All Hardly ever swears a big, big D!
          Then give three cheers, and one cheer more,
          For the well-bred Captain of the *Pinafore*!
          Then give three cheers and one cheer more,
          For the Captain of the *Pinafore*!
Carte I can't see the show going during this heat. (*He takes off the Captain's hat and jacket*)
Sullivan No, the summer was a bad time to open.
Carte I can't see us surviving the season.
Gilbert Nonsense, Carte, don't worry.
Carte But Gilbert, the Board are very concerned.
Gilbert As I keep saying. Bugger the Board, keep going. (*He takes the hat and jacket*)

Carte exits

First Lord, Captain and Josephine

Captain (Gilbert) Never mind the why and wherefore,
          Love can level ranks, and therefore,
          Though his lordship's station's mighty,
              Though stupendous be his brain,
          Though her tastes are mean and flighty
              And her fortunes poor and plain.
Captain ⎱ Ring the merry bells on board-ship
Sir Joseph ⎰   Rend the air with warbling wild,
          For the union of ⁽ʰⁱˢ⁾ lordship
                          ⁽ᵐʸ⁾
          With a humble captain's child!
Captain For a humble captain's daughter—
Josephine (Sybil) For a gallant captain's daughter—
Sir Joseph And a lord who rules the water—
Josephine (*aside*) And a *tar* who ploughs the water—
All Let the air with joy be laden,
          Rend with songs the air above,
          For the union of a maiden
              With the man who owns her love!

Dance

Sir Joseph Never mind the why and wherefore
　　　Love can level ranks, and therefore.

　Carte enters

Carte Er—Gilbert . . .
Gilbert Don't tell me. Trouble with the Board again.
Carte 'Fraid so.
Gilbert What is it this time?
Carte They want to take it off.
Gilbert *H.M.S. Pinafore?*
All Oh no!
Carte I'm sorry.
Gilbert The bloody fools!
Carte I know. I know.
Gilbert But they can't take it off.
Carte The box office takings have been very low. It's this hot weather.
Gilbert This is England. The hot weather can't last.
Carte If only we could survive these few weeks until the autumn. Believe
　　me, Gilbert, I've done my best to make them see sense. I've told them
　　also that if they do take it off it will be the death of English comic opera.
Gilbert I give up. Can't you do something?
Carte Really, Gilbert. My head's on the block. If they take off *Pinafore*,
　　I'm finished.

Gilbert shrugs "Well, that's it"

Sullivan I've got it.
Gilbert (*sarcastically*) What shall we do, dedicate it to the Prince of Wales?
Sullivan No—no—I mean it. I'm conducting at the promenade concert
　　tonight. Leave it to me.

*Sullivan goes to the podium to conduct. Placards are held up by the Stage
Hands—PINAFORE MANIA: TOURS BEGIN: WHAT NEVER?:
HARDLY EVER: 10,000 PIANO SCORES SOLD DAILY. The singers,
including Sullivan, take their places*

Sir Joseph Never mind the why and wherefore,
　　　Love can level ranks and therefore,
　　　Though your nautical relation (*alluding to the Captain*)
　　　　In my set could scarcely pass—
　　　Though you occupy a station
　　　　In the lower middle class

Placards are held up

Captain ⎱　Ring the merry bells on board-ship,
Sir Joseph ⎰　　Rend the air with warbling wild,
　　　For the union of $\begin{smallmatrix}\text{(his)}\\\text{(my)}\end{smallmatrix}$ lordship
　　　With a humble captain's child!

Captain For a humble captain's daughter—
Josephine For a gallant captain's daughter—
Sir Joseph And a lord who rules the water—
Josephine (*aside*) And a *tar* who ploughs the water!
All Let the air with joy be laden,
    Rend with songs the air above,
    For the union of a maiden
      With the man who owns her love!

Dance

Josephine Never mind the why and wherefore
    Love can level ranks, and therefore
Carte Gilbert . . .

Gilbert glares at Carte and can hardly speak

  (*Shrugging, smiling*) I know, I know.
Gilbert You tell that damned and blasted Board that I have had a gut full
  of the whole lot of them . . .
Sullivan And so have I. Let's buy them out . . .
Gilbert You tell them that I'll come down personally and wring—their . . .
  What was that, Sullivan?
Sullivan We can buy them out.
Gilbert (*to Carte*) Are you with us?
Carte Right behind you.
Gilbert Fix it up. Tell them we want them out in one month from today—
  that's when the contract expires. From then on they'll have no further
  claim on our work or on our properties.
Carte There may be reprisals, they are ruthless.
Gilbert We'll handle any reprisals.

Carte turns away. The piano starts "Why and Wherefore". Sybil begins to
sing "Never mind". Carte turns round carrying a travelling-bag

Gilbert (*to Sybil*) Be quiet. Where are you going, Carte? You can't run
  out on us now.
Carte I'm going to America. *Pinafore* is sweeping the States. It's a forest
  fire. Your words are on everyone's lips. On every street corner barrel-
  organs are churning out Sullivan's music.
Sullivan Barrel-organs?
Gilbert And we're not making a penny out of it. Can't you do something?
Carte I'm going to America myself. You take care of things whilst I'm
  away. On my return we'll fix up a new contract. But watch out for the
  Board, they threatened to stop performances.
Josephine Never mind the why and wherefore,
    Love can level ranks, and therefore
    I admit the jurisdiction;
      Ably have you played your part;
    You have carried firm conviction
      To my hesitating heart . . .

The song peters out, and the Lights fade to a Black-out. Sound of fight going on. Jessie comes forward with a candle

Jessie Ladies and gentlemen. We've had a slight brush with the Board who have tried to steal our properties. But we have routed them! The company is now ours, so on with the show!

Cheers. The Lights come up. The piano starts the intro of "Never mind the Why and Wherefore" but is interrupted by Carte

Carte I've fixed it! I've done it! I have done a deal with the Americans! We're going to put on the authorised version of *Pinafore* in New York. We're all going to America!

Cheers

Josephine (*determined*) Never mind the why and wherefore,
    Love can level ranks, and therefore
I admit the jurisdiction
    Ably have you played your part;
You have carried firm conviction
    To my hesitating heart
Sullivan Very nice.
Captain ⎫ Ring the merry bells on board-ship,
Sir Joseph ⎭   Rend the air with warbling wild,
    For the union of $\frac{(his)}{(my)}$ lordship
With a humble captain's child!
Captain For a humble captain's daughter—
Josephine (*Sybil*) For a gallant captain's daughter—
Sir Joseph And a lord who rules the water—
Josephine (*aside*) And a tar who ploughs the water—
    (*Aloud*) Let the air with joy be laden.
Captain ⎫
Sir Joseph ⎭ Ring the merry bells on board-ship
Josephine For the union of a maiden—
Captain ⎫
Sir Joseph ⎭ For her union with his lordship.
All Rend with songs the air above
    For the man who owns her love!

The Company breaks up

The contract between Gilbert and Sullivan and Carte is to be signed. Carte moves above the table, Gilbert and Sullivan to either side. Helen (Geraldine) joins them

Carte Well, gentlemen, we have rid ourselves of the Board. We are now our own masters. This is the contract I propose, from the date of the withdrawal of *H.M.S. Pinafore*. We shall each of us contribute trading capital—at present, let us say a thousand pounds each, now we shall

review the situation periodically and adjust accordingly, but this will
form the basis of the agreement.

Gilbert It says here the profits will be divided *after* all expenses have been
deducted.

Carte That is fair.

Gilbert And who is to do the accounting?

Carte Helen will see that you are given a complete run down.

Gilbert And we'll have to stick to this for five years?

Carte Yes.

Gilbert signs

Thank you. Arthur.

Gilbert passes the contract to Sullivan, who peruses the document

Don't let this business hold us up, gentlemen. I mean here to protect
us. We must move sharply now and take our own company to do
Pinafore the way *we* want to do it in New York. We must take the
fight right into the pirate's camp. They are robbing us of thousands a
week . . .

Gilbert Better still, we'll open our new show in New York. Much of the
writing's finished. A lot of the music is ready. We'll rehearse it out
there.   9a

Piano—"Poor Wandering One"

Carte Splendid idea. You are far enough advanced to do that? Is it exciting?

Gilbert Very exciting.

Carte Colourful?

Gilbert Very colourful.

Carte Songs? Pleasant songs?

Gilbert The music is . . .

Carte Come on, Arthur, sign.

Sullivan turns to look towards Mabel (Sybil), who has approached

THE PIRATES OF PENZANCE

Mabel (Sybil) For shame, for shame, for shame!

SONG

Poor wandering one!   9a
Though thou has surely strayed,
  Take heart of grace,
  Thy steps retrace,
Poor wandering one!
Poor wandering one!
If such poor love as mine

Can help thee find
True peace of mind—
Why, take it, it is thine!

Gilbert Aren't you going to sign, Sullivan? To make everything legal between us.

Sullivan Yes, and binding.

Carte We are not going to give offence in this opera, are we? We don't want another Pinafore-Smith!   **9b**

Gilbert Well, we do have this military chap in it, but—

Piano—"A Modern Major-General"

I don't think he'll give offence.

Carte What never?

Gilbert Well . . . No, he won't give offence . . .

Major-General (Grossmith) replaces Mabel

SONG—MAJOR-GENERAL

General (Grossmith) I am the very model of a modern Major-General,
I've information vegetable, animal, and mineral,
I know the kings of England, and I quote the fights historical,
From Marathon to Waterloo, in order categorical—
I'm very well acquainted too with matters mathematical,
I understand equations, both the simple and quadratical,
About binomial theorem I'm teeming with a lot of news—

I haven't finished yet, what comes after that?

Gilbert Hypotenuse.

General Oh yes, quite right.
With many cheerful facts about the square of the hypotenuse
For my military knowledge, though I'm plucky and adventury,
Has only been brought down to the beginning of the century;
But still in matters vegetable, animal, and mineral,
I am the very model of a modern Major-General.

Carte Got a title for it yet, Gilbert?

Gilbert We're going to fight the pirates with a play about pirates . . . so we'll call it the *Pirates* . . .

Carte Just the *Pirates*?

Gilbert No—let me see. We'll call it the—

The piano starts

—*Pirates of Penzance.*

Carte Ah! *The Pirates of Penzance.*

Joe enters, dressed as an odd-looking pirate

SONG—PIRATE KING

Oh, better far to live and die
Under the brave black flag I fly,
Than play a sanctimonious part,
With a pirate head and a pirate heart.
Away to the cheating world go you,
Where pirates all are well-to-do;
But I'll be true to the song I sing,
And live and die a Pirate King.
    For I am a Pirate King.

    And it is, it is a glorious thing
    To be a Pirate King!
(Repeat the last two lines)
    Hurrah for the Pirate King.

The Stage Hands bring on luggage and other impedimenta for a journey and start preparations

Gilbert That's it, let's get moving.

Carte It will be a challenge in America. But if we pull it off . . .

Gilbert They started the fight. They threw down the challenge. They're going to end up with bloody noses. . . .

Carte It's not going to be easy, though. That's why we need to be united. Arthur, you still haven't signed.

Gilbert What is the matter with you, Sullivan. Cold feet?

Carte Now, don't cause a fuss. (*Soothingly*) Now, Arthur, old chap, just sign and let us get this business out of the way.

Sullivan Five years is a long time for a serious composer to commit himself to comic opera.

Gilbert Look, don't underrate these comic operas. They are good pieces of work, and what is more they've already earned you far more money than any of your so-called serious stuff, so don't throw stones at them. You'll not catch Carte throwing stones. Will you?

Carte Me? No. Never . . .

Gilbert What never?

Carte Well, not yet.

Piano—"Tarantara!"

Sullivan slowly picks up his pen

Come on, Arthur, sign. I'll have a word with Gilbert. But America will put him in his place. It is you they are waiting to meet out there. Just sign there. No more petty squabbling. There is money to be earned. And a common enemy to fight. We're going to *America*!

All the bags are packed ready

Joe Don't forget your baton.

The Men pick up various bags. The Girls line up with them, ready to march

SONG—SERGEANT

9d
(cont.)

Sergeant (Carte) When the foeman bares his steel,
    Tarantara! tarantara!
We uncomfortable feel,
    Tarantara!
And we find the wisest thing,
    Tarantara! tarantara!
Is to slap our chests and sing
    Tarantara!
For when threatened with emeutes,
    Tarantara! tarantara!
And your heart is in your boots,
    Tarantara!
There is nothing brings it round
Like the trumpet's martial sound,
  (*Repeat line*)
    Tarantara! tarantara!
    Tarantara-ra-ra-ra-ra!
All Tarantara-ra-ra-ra-ra!
  (*Refer to score*)
Mabel (Sybil) Go, ye heroes, go to glory,
    Though you die in combat gory,
    Ye shall live in song and story.
      Go to immortality!
    Go to death, and go to slaughter;
    Die, and every Cornish daughter
    With her tears your grave shall water.
    Go, ye heroes, go and die.
      Go, ye heroes, go and die!
Girls Go, ye heroes, go and die!
Police (Gilbert) Though to us it's evident,
    Tarantara! tarantara!
These attentions are well meant,
    Tarantara!
Such expressions don't appear,
    Tarantara! tarantara!
Calculated men to cheer,
    Tarantara!
Who are going to meet their fate
In a highly nervous state,
    Tarantara! Tarantara! Tarantara!
Still to us it's evident
These attentions are well meant.
    Tarantara! Tarantara! Tarantara!

Edith (Jessie) Go and do your best endeavour,
    And before all links we sever,
    We will say farewell for ever.
        Go to glory and the grave! Go to glory and the grave!
Girls For your foes are fierce and ruthless,
    False, unmerciful, and truthless.
    Young and tender, old and toothless,
        All in vain their mercy crave.
Sergeant (Sullivan) We observe too great a stress,
    On the risks that on us press,
    And of reference a lack
    To our chance of coming back.
    Still, perhaps it would be wise
    Not to carp or criticize,
    For it's very evident
    These attentions are well meant.
Men Yes it's very evident
    These attentions are well meant
    Evident, yes well meant,
    Evident, ah yes, well meant.

SONG—SERGEANT

Sergeant (Carte) When the foeman bares his steel,
    Tarantara! tarantara!
    We uncomfortable feel,
    Tarantara!
    And we find the wisest thing,
    Tarantara! tarantara!
    Is to slap our chests and sing
    Tarantara!
    For when threatened with émeutes,
    Tarantara! tarantara!
    And your heart is in your boots,
    Tarantara!
    There is nothing brings it round,
    Like the trumpet's martial sound,
  (*Repeat*)
    Tarantara! tarantara!
    Tarantara-ra-ra-ra-ra!
All Tarantara-ra-ra-ra-ra! (*See score*)
Mabel Go, ye heroes, go to glory,
    Though ye die in combat gory,
    Ye shall live in song and story
        Go to immortality!
    Go to death, and go to slaughter;
    Die, and every Cornish daughter

With her tears your grave shall water.
Go, ye heroes, go to immortality
Girls Go, ye heroes, go and die!
Go, ye heroes, go to immortality
Though ye die in combat gory
Ye shall live in song and story.
Mabel Go to immortality.
Edith Away, away!
Police (*without moving*) Yes, yes, we go.
Edith These pirates slay.
Police Tarantara!
Edith Then do not stay,
Police Tarantara!
Edith Then why this delay?
Police All right—we go.
Yes, forward on the foe!
(*Repeat—see score*)
Edith Yes, but you don't go!
Police We go, we go!
Yes, forward on the foe!
(*Repeat*)
Edith Yes, but you don't go!
(*See score*)
Police We go!
Girls At last they really go.

The Men march off, as—

the CURTAIN *falls*

ACT II

The Company are discovered performing an extract from "Patience". The lovesick maidens (Jessie, Sybil and Geraldine) are fawning over Bunthorne (Gilbert)

Girls Twenty love-sick maidens we,
　　Love-sick all against our will.
　　Twenty years hence we shall be—
　　Twenty love-sick maidens still.

Enter the chorus of Dragoons, marching briskly

Men The soldiers of our Queen
　　Are linked in friendly tether;
　　Upon the battle scene
　　They fight the foe together.
　　There every mother's son
　　Prepared to fight and fall is;
　　The enemy of one
　　The enemy of all is!
(Repeat the last two lines)
Colonel (Sullivan) Stand at ease!

SONG—COLONEL

　When I first put this uniform on,
　　I said, as I looked in the glass,
　　　"It's one to a million
　　　That any civilian
　　My figure and form will surpass.
　　Gold lace has a charm for the fair,
　　And I've plenty of that, and to spare,
　　　While a lover's professions,
　　　When uttered in Hessians,
　　Are eloquent everywhere!"
　　　A fact that I counted upon,
　　　When I first put this uniform on!

CHORUS OF DRAGOONS

Men By a simple coincidence, few
      Could ever have counted upon,
    The same thing occurred to me, too,
      When I first put this uniform on!
Colonel I said, when I first put it on,
      "It is plain to the veriest dunce,
        That every beauty
        Will feel it her duty,
    To yield to its glamour at once.
They will see that I'm freely gold-laced
In a uniform handsome and chaste"—
      But the peripatetics
      Of long-haired aesthetics
Are very much more to their taste—
      Which I never counted upon,
      When I first put this uniform on!
Men By a simple coincidence, few
      Could ever have reckoned upon,
    I didn't anticipate that,
      When I first put this uniform on!

The Men exit. Bunthorne dismisses the Girls

Girls Oh no! Not that.

Bunthorne is adamant and strikes a pose

The Girls exit

Bunthorne (Gilbert) Am I alone and unobserved? I am.
    Then let me own. I'm an aesthetic sham.

SONG

    If you're anxious for to shine in the high
      aesthetic line as a man of culture rare,
    You must get up all the germs of the transcendental
      terms, and plant them everywhere.
    You must lie upon the daisies and discourse in novel
      phrases of your complicated state of mind,
    The meaning doesn't matter if it's only idle
      chatter of a transcendental kind.
        And every one will say,
        As you walk your mystic way,
    "If this young man expresses himself in terms
      too deep for *me*,

Why, what a very singularly deep young man this
   deep young man must be!''
Then a sentimental passion of a vegetable fashion
   must excite your languid spleen,
An attachment à la Plato for a bashful young
   potato, or a not-too French french bean!
Though the Philistines may jostle, you will rank
   as an apostle in the high aesthetic band,
If you walk down Piccadilly with a poppy or a lily
   in your mediaeval hand.
      And every one will say,
      As you walk your flowery way,
"If he's content with a vegetable love which would
   certainly not suit me,
Why, what a most particularly pure young man
   this pure young man must be!''

*Gilbert exits. Joe enters, followed by all except Gilbert. They gather round
Carte's table*

Joe Summer eighteen eighty-one. Richard D'Oyly is basking in the finan-
cial and aesthetic glow of *Patience*, and momentarily secure in the knowledge that his two protagonists are not yet at each other's throats, he
holds a press conference.

Reporter (Geraldine) Of course, Mr Carte, in *Patience*, Gilbert and Sullivan
are attacking the Art world.

Carte In satirizing the excesses of the so-called aesthetes the authors of
Patience have not desired to cast ridicule on the true aesthetic spirit, but
only to attack unmanly oddities which masquerade in its likeness.

Reporter (Grossmith) Come on, Mr Carte, they are knocking Oscar Wilde,
aren't they?

Carte Not at all. Mr Gilbert has every respect for Mr Wilde both as an
artist and as a personality. It is the imitators of Mr Wilde that he is
attacking.

Reporter (Sybil) Has Oscar Wilde made any comments on *Patience*?

Carte He has seen it twice and he laughed a good deal. In fact, he told
me personally how much he enjoyed it. And to show that there is no ill
will between us, he is shortly to do a lecture tour of the United States
for me . . .

Reporter (Jessie) Oh. You are sending him out, before the touring company, as an advertisement.

Carte Well, I could hire sandwich-board men with uncut hair much more
cheaply.

Reporter (Joe) Mr Carte, there are rumours of a new project in the air.

Carte Yes, I intend to house my new operettas . . .

Reporters (All) In a new theatre?

Carte On the site of the old Savoy Palace. It will seat over one thousand
and two hundred persons. And instead of the usual foul-smelling gas

lamps, I intend to install a new electric light . . .

Joe exits and re-enters immediately with an electric light bulb on a cushion, and a hammer

Reporters (All) Electric light?

Gilbert enters

Carte I just happen to have a bulb here. (*He holds up the bulb and hammer*) Much cleaner. Much brighter. And certainly much safer. I will demonstrate.
Gilbert Hold on there. Are you personally financing this venture?

All but Gilbert and Carte exit

Carte Yes.
Gilbert By our agreement we share profits and costs. Electricity is going to put the costs up.
Carte Yes, but the box office takings will be much greater. Believe me, Gilbert, I know what I am doing. Supposing we draw up a new agreement, whereby we each of us pay four thousand pounds per year rent.
Gilbert You mean you as partner will pay yourself as landlord one-third of the rent?
Carte Yes.
Gilbert You've made a very good investment there, Carte, you can't lose, but I don't think it will be much good to Sullivan and I . . .
Carte Gilbert, you are already earning over ten thousand per year. That's more than the Prime Minister gets.
Gilbert I bring more pleasure to people than the Prime Minister does.

Sullivan enters and sits on his podium

Carte And what about that *new* luxury palace you are building in Kensington—with all those bathrooms . . .?
Gilbert At least I don't gamble it all away like Sullivan—this won't do, Carte. I'll ring Sullivan on my *new* telephone.

A golden light comes up on Sullivan. Ladies cluster around him offering chocolates, mopping his brow, etc.

Sullivan (*in the sun*) You can't.
Gilbert Why not?
Sullivan Firstly I'm not there—secondly I'm not on the telephone.
Gilbert Where are you?
Sullivan I'm cruising in the Baltic with Alfie.
Gilbert Alfie?
Sullivan Duke of Edinburgh.
Gilbert I might have known.

Sullivan Oh, by the by, the King of Denmark looked after us frightfully well.

Gilbert Really? I'm so glad.

Sullivan And I have never tasted food like the Tsar gave us.

Gilbert Fascinating.

Sullivan Oh, and when I met Prince Wilhelm, he bowed and sang, "He polished op ze hondle on ze big front door". We all roared, it was too funny.

Gilbert What a riot. Perhaps after your cruise, you wouldn't mind sparing some thought to business, Carte is opening a new theatre . . .

Sullivan I know, I know.

Gilbert With electric lamps burning all over the place.

Sullivan Very bright and cheerful.

Gilbert He's going to charge us four thousand pounds per year rent.

Sullivan Mmmm. Well, all in all, it's pretty fair.

Gilbert And I have the plot of our new comic opera ready.

Sullivan Aha.

Carte Splendid.

The golden light fades

The Ladies exit

Gilbert and Sullivan stand on either side of Carte

Gilbert —So, you see, the old crone swallows the lozenge . . .

Sullivan Excuse me. Pardon me . . . Swallows?

Carte A lozenge, Sullivan.

Sullivan Ahh. Continue.

Gilbert She swallows a lozenge and right away becomes a ravishing beauty, young, sweet, pretty, hmmmph?

Sullivan Hmmmmm.

Carte Sounds very nice—good.

Gilbert Now the young woman swallows a lozenge . . .

Sullivan And she becomes an old woman.

Gilbert That's it, you've got it.

Sullivan And the handsome hero, you mentioned, he swallows a lozenge——

Carte (*excitedly*) —and he becomes an old man.

Gilbert Exactly . . .

Carte And you have an old man who swallows this—this——

Sullivan —lozenge——

Carte —lozenge—and he becomes——

Sullivan —a young man—and you have a good man and he swallows this lozenge and he becomes evil—and you have an evil man who becomes good—a cat who becomes a dog—and so on and so on—all swallowing lozenges . . .

Carte Yes, yes.

Gilbert Yes, yes.

Sullivan And everything goes topsy-turvy again.

Gilbert Yes. Do you like it?
Sullivan No.
Gilbert Why not?
Sullivan It's a lot of nonsense. What we want is realism.
Carte Yes, yes. Lozenges are all very well, Gilbert. But we do want realism.
Gilbert Carte, what are you blathering about? Just because Sullivan has realism on the brain—not that I think he knows what it means—do you have to parrot him? "What we want is realism." Do you think these plots grow on trees?
Carte No, but I just think that we could fill the bill nicely with something a little more realistic.
Gilbert Do you realize that while you have been gadding about the Continent, I have been sweating blood to get this plot right. My gout's ten times worse. I have not been to bed for a fortnight. And God knows how many more sleepless nights this is going to cost me.
Carte (*going to sit at his table*) Oh, but you'll get it, Gilbert old man. You always do.

Gilbert sits at his desk

Sullivan Look. Let me know when you come up with something. I must dash now, Carte. So much work has piled up while I've been away. Do you mind if I use your telephone? (*He does so*) Mayfair two-six-oh, please. . . . Mrs Ronalds, please. . . . Hello, Mary. . . .
Gilbert Hello, Mary.
Sullivan Sorry to have kept you. . . . I'm on my way now. 'Bye. . . . (*He replaces the receiver*) Cheer up, Gilbert. Try and get some sleep.

Grossmith enters

Gilbert Sleep—sleep! (*He leans over the desk and tries to sleep*)

Piano

NIGHTMARE SONG   11

Lord Chancellor (Grossmith)
When you're lying awake with a dismal headache,
   and repose is tabooed by anxiety
I conceive you may use any language you choose to indulge
   in without impropriety
For your brain is on fire—the bedclothes conspire
   of usual slumber to plunder you.
First your counterpane goes, and uncovers your toes,
   and your sheet slips demurely from under you.
Then the blanketing tickles—you feel like mixed pickles—
   so terribly sharp is the pricking
And you're hot and you're cross, and you tumble and
   toss till there's nothing twixt you and the ticking

Then the bedclothes all creep to the ground in a heap,
   and you pick 'em all up in a tangle
Next your pillow resigns and politely declines to remain
   at its usual angle.
Well you get some repose in the form of a doze, with
   hot eyeballs and head ever aching.
But your slumbering teems with such horrible dreams
   that you'd very much better be waking
For you dream you are crossing the Channel and tossing
   about in a steamer from Harwich
Which is something between a large bathing machine and
   a very small second-class carriage
And you're giving a treat (penny ice and cold meat) to
   a party of friends and relations.
They're a ravenous horde—and they all come on board at
   Sloane Square and South Kensington Stations.
And bound on that journey you find your attorney (who
   started that morning from Devon)
He's a bit undersized and you don't feel surprised
   when he tells you he's only eleven.
Well you're driving like mad with this singular lad
   by the by the ship's now a four-wheeler
And you are playing round games and he calls you bad
   names when you tell him that ties pays the dealer
But this you can't stand, so you throw up your hand,
   and you find you're as cold as an icicle
In your shirt and your socks (the black silk with
   gold clocks) crossing Salisbury Plain on a bicycle
And he and his crew are on bicycles too—which they've
   somehow or other invested in—
And he's telling the tars all the particulars of a
   company he's interested in
It's a scheme of devices to get at low prices all goods from
   cough mixtures to cables
(Which tickled the sailors) by treating retailers
   as though they were all vegetables
You get a good spadesman to plant a small tradesman
   (first take off his boots with a boot tree)
And his legs will take root, and his fingers will shoot,
   and they'll blossom and bud like a fruit tree—
From the greengrocer tree you get grapes and green pea,
   cauliflower, pineapple and cranberries
While the pastrycook plant cherry brandy will grant
   apple puffs and three corners and Banbury's.
The shares are a penny, and ever so many are taken by
   Rothschild and Baring
And just as a few are allotted to you, you awake with a
   shudder despairing—

You're a regular wreck, with a crick in your neck,
and no wonder you snore, for your head's on the floor,
and you've needles and pins from your soles to your
shins, and your flesh is a-creep, for your left leg's
asleep and you've cramp in your toes, and a fly in your
nose, and some fluff in your lung, and a feverish tongue,
and a thirst that's intense, and a general sense that you
haven't been sleeping in clover;
But the darkness has passed and it's daylight at last,
and the night has been long—ditto ditto my song—
and thank goodness they're both of them over.

Lord Chancellor taps Gilbert on the shoulder to wake him, and then exits

Gilbert slams his desk

Gilbert I've got it. I've got it all worked out. It's about this chap who's a fairy—but only from the waist up. He goes into Parliament and runs amok in the House of Lords. There's a chorus of Peers and a chorus of fairies—Lord Chancellor—ideal for Grossmith. (*He writes feverishly*)

Grossmith enters and crosses behind Gilbert

Carte sits at his table. Sullivan and Grossmith move to it

Grossmith Mr Carte, Mr Sullivan.
Carte Just a minute, George.
Grossmith Mr Sullivan, I'm still very worried about the Nightmare song.
Sullivan Don't worry, George, just do it as you did it in rehearsal. On a first night nobody's going to know if you get the words right or not!
Grossmith Mr Gilbert will.
Sullivan He won't be in.
Grossmith No, no, he won't. No, he never is on a first night. Why's that?
Sullivan He can't face them.
Grossmith What? Mr Gilbert?
Carte He's more nervous than you are. He spends his time walking up and down the Embankment, or at his Club until it is time for him to come and take his curtain call . . .
Carte Is everything all right now, George?
Grossmith Yes thank you, Mr Carte. I feel a lot better now. Good luck, Mr Sullivan. (*He starts to go*)
Sullivan Good luck, George.

Carte waves

Grossmith exits

Carte Now then, Arthur, what is it? You look terrible.
Sullivan I feel terrible. (*He sits by the table*) I ache and I'm in pain and I can't get anything to soothe it.

Carte I was very sorry to hear about your mother.

Sullivan It is not only that. Look, Carte, can I tell you something very confidential?

Carte Yes.

Sullivan Don't tell anybody, not even Gilbert. Especially Gilbert. Carte, I am financially ruined, cleaned out.

Carte Gambling?

Sullivan No. Not at the tables, anyhow. (*Producing a paper*) Look, this arrived just as I was leaving for the theatre this evening.

Carte (*taking the paper and reading*) Cooper and Hall . . .

Sullivan My brokers. They've gone bankrupt. Every penny I had in the world was with them. It has all gone.

Carte But surely you must have other resources.

Sullivan No—nothing. I can't take much more, Carte. I feel old and tired and on top of everything there's Gilbert. I'm beginning to dread working with him. He deliberately refuses to feed me the kind of material I desperately need. Carte, when I go through crises like this, I feel terrified, I suddenly realize how short life is. Carte, I must achieve something before I die . . .

Carte You shall, I'll help you all I can. I cannot say more than that at present. I do realize how you must be feeling . . .

Sullivan Do you? I wonder. (*Rising*) I'm sorry, I didn't mean that, it's just that I have to pay heavily for my pleasures. And when troubles come—I'd like to escape from it all.

Jessie enters, followed by Sybil and Geraldine. Joe follows with jacket and bearskin for Sullivan

Fairy Queen (Jessie) Private Willis.   12

Piano

Sentry (Sullivan) Ma'am.

Queen To save my life it is necessary that I marry at once. How would you like to be a Fairy Guardsman?

Sentry Well, ma'am, I don't think much of a British soldier who wouldn't ill-convenience himself to save a female in distress.

Queen You are a brave fellow. You are a fairy from this moment! And how say you, my lords? Will you join our ranks?

Lord Mount (Gilbert) Well, now that the Peers are to be recruited from persons of intelligence I don't see what use we are down here, do you, Tolloller?

Tolloller (Carte) None whatsoever.   13

Queen Good! Then away we go to Fairyland.

  Soon as we may off and away.

IOLANTHE

SONG—

Girls Soon as we may,
    Off and away!
We'll commence our journey airy—
    Happy are we—
    As you can see,
Everyone is now a fairy!
All Every, every, every, every, everyone is now a fairy!
Iolanthe (Sybil) Though as a general rule we know
Queen Two strings go to every bow,
Phyl (Geraldine) Make up your minds that grief 'twill bring.
    If you've two beaux to every string.
Lord Chancellor Up in the sky,
    Ever so high,
Pleasures come in endless series;
    We will arrange
    Happy exchange—
House of Peers to House of Peris!
All Peris, Peris, Peris
    House of Peers to House of Peris!
Lord Chancellor Up in the air, sky-high, sky-high,
       Free from Wards in Chancery,

Mount   (I)
Tolloller (He) will be surely happier, for
       (I'm)
       (He) such a susceptible Chancellor.

    (*Repeat "Up in the air . . ." until interrupted*)
Critic 1 (Jessie) Where is this topsy-turveydom going to end?
Critic 2 (Grossmith) I'd rather watch a Punch and Judy show.
Critic 1 Doesn't come within a mile of *Pinafore*.

Joe enters with a tray of champagne glasses which he hands round

Critic 1 Sullivan is a masterly musician, but he's sacrificing himself to
    Gilbert . . .
Joe Thirteenth May eighteen eighty-three. Dr Sullivan is forty-one today.
    He is giving a cocktail party. Everyone who is anyone is here—the lead-
    ing critics—Prince of Wales—Mrs Ronalds . . . Mr Carte. And even
    Mr Gilbert is enjoying himself.
American Woman (Sybil) (*having trailed Gilbert*) Wonderful man, your Dr
    Sullivan.
Gilbert Yes, wonderful.
American Woman His music is so very popular all over the United States.
    You know, Mr Ahhh . . .
Gilbert Gilbert.

American Woman Oh yes, Mr Gilbert, yes. You are so very lucky to have the privilege of knowing and working with him.

Gilbert Yes, it's very sacrificial of him to allow it to happen.

American Woman Pardon me?

Gilbert It is always an education working with a great composer.

American Woman I'm sure it is, I am sure it is. You know, in America we have nothing like your European composers—we just love your European composers. Have you met many of them?

Gilbert Oh, one comes across 'em, you know, in odd places.

American Woman Oh, you're so lucky—Mr Gilbey . . .

Gilbert Gilbert.

American Woman Mr Gilbert, Mr Baych, Joe-Ann Sebaystian Baych, he is still composing?

Gilbert No, madam, I think not, at present I believe he is by way of decomposing . . .

A Waiter (Joe) Ladies and gentlemen, it is now nine-thirty . . .

Sullivan I want you all to come and listen to my telephone.

All except Gilbert show delight

Joe collects the glasses and exits

Mrs Ronalds (Geraldine) Oh, Mr Gilbert, you mustn't miss our surprise, we are just about to go through and listen into the telephone! To hear the second act of *Iolanthe* right from the stage of the Savoy . . .

Gilbert It's hardly a surprise for me, I am able to do that whenever I please.

Mrs Ronalds But it will be a thrill for my friends, don't you think?

Gilbert Possibly, Mrs Ronalds, possibly, but I'd find it even more thrilling if they were to buy tickets for tomorrow night's performance. Good night, Mrs Ronalds.

Gilbert exits

Joe enters with a note on a salver for Sullivan

Sullivan Mary, the Prince of Wales has just congratulated me, but I do not know for what.

Mrs Ronalds Well may I be the second to congratulate you, whatever it is . . .

Sullivan (*opening the note*) It's from Mr Gladstone . . .

Piano—"National Anthem"   1

Gladstone (Grossmith) I am permitted by Her Majesty to propose that in recognition of your distinguished talents as a composer . . .

Piano—"March of Peers"

A Stage Hand brings on a sword for Jessie

The Stage Hand exits with the sword

Critic (Sybil) Sir Arthur, show yourself the best man in Europe.
Critic (Geraldine) Sir Arthur, how long is it since you composed anything worthy of you?
Critic (Sybil) Sir Arthur, your friends have to apologize for you.
Critic (Geraldine) Sir Arthur, you were knighted to shame you into writing something better than these silly comic operas with that wretched Gilbert.
Critic (Grossmith) Some things Dr Sullivan may do, Sir Arthur Sullivan may not do . . .
Critic (Jessie) It will look very odd to read that a new comic opera is in preparation by W. S. Gilbert and Sir Arthur Sullivan.

All exit except Joe and Sullivan

Sullivan goes to sit on the podium

Joe We regret to announce that Sir Arthur Sullivan fainted when he presented himself on the stage of the Savoy last night to receive the congratulations of the audience for *Princess Ida*. The following bulletin has been posted: "Sir Arthur has passed a quiet night, and although in pain he is on the whole better. Absolute rest and quietude has been enjoined by his doctors."

Joe exits

Sullivan Hmmm.

Carte enters and goes to his table. Geraldine (as Helen) enters and gives him a letter

Helen It's from Sullivan.
Carte Oh, good, I hope he's feeling better now.

Carte peruses the letter with growing consternation

Sullivan I regret to have to inform you that I am not going to write any more music for comic opera . . .

Carte looks across at Helen

Helen I've been expecting it.
Carte Oh, he must be tired, after being so ill. But we'd better go and see him. The *Princess Ida* receipts are dropping already.
Helen Yes, but I should go easy with him. It may be more serious than you think it is.

Helen and Carte go to Sullivan, who rises

It's good to see you looking so much better, Arthur.

Carte Yes, worried about you, Arthur. Very worried . . .

Sullivan Well I'm in less pain now. A rest and a trip away will put me right, and then I can start to think about the future . . .

Helen A good idea . . .

Carte But there is of course, the question . . .

Helen (*quickly*) Where are you going?

Sullivan I thought I might go to Paris for a while and then on to Brussels . . .

Helen It's good to get away and forget everything . . .

Sullivan (*guiltily*) I'm sorry about my letter, Richard.

Carte Oh, I can understand how you feel, Arthur, you've been under such tremendous pressure. Don't worry, *Princess Ida* will hold up for a few weeks until you are feeling better. Gilbert is already working on a new libretto . . .

Sullivan It won't concern me.

Carte (*with a smile*) I refuse to take you seriously at the moment . . .

Sullivan That is my last word. No more comic opera. (*He sits*)

Carte We'll see. We'll see . . .

Helen and Carte move back to the table

He must write another score. He is under contract.

Helen And *Princess Ida* will have to come off soon. And we have nothing to take its place.

Carte We'd better write to Sullivan. Where is he now?

Helen Brussels.

She picks up a pad and pencil, and sits. Carte dictates a letter to her

Carte "Business, as you will have observed, shows signs of falling off. By our arrangement I have to give you six months' notice in case of a new piece being required. Please accept this note as fulfilling the necessary formality. I have already sent a copy of this note to Gilbert.'

Helen exits. Gilbert enters, reading a note

Sullivan (*writing to Carte*) "My dear Carte, it is *impossible* for me to do another piece of those already written by Gilbert and myself . . ."

Gilbert (*writing to Sullivan*) "Dear Sullivan, I am amazed at your attitude. You are aware by our five-year agreement we are *bound* to supply Carte with a new opera on receiving from him six months' notice, and, if we fail to do so we are liable to him for any losses that may result from our default . . ."

Sullivan (*writing to Gilbert*) "With *Princess Ida*, I came to the end of my tether with that kind of piece. The music is never allowed to speak for itself."

Gilbert (*writing to Sullivan*) "Your reflections on the character of the libretto I have supplied you with causes me much pain. I enclose a new libretto.

Sullivan (*reading*) ". . . and the hero, a mountebank, swallows a . . . (*he drops the script*) lozenge . . ." Don't you see? I'm tired of all that. We must break new ground. Don't you see? I want something of importance to work on.

Gilbert, having thought it over, telephones Sullivan, who lifts his receiver

Gilbert Sullivan, I'm completely at a loss to know what you want from me. The best thing to do is find someone else to write a libretto for you . . .

Sullivan Simply because your libretto does not seem to furnish me suitable musical suggestion, doesn't mean we should grind to a standstill . . .

Gilbert Find someone else, damn you!

Off-stage voices are heard

Jessie (*off*) Sir Arthur Sullivan and Mr Gilbert look like splitting for the simple reason that they cannot find a story.

Grossmith (*off*) The great question of the day is: Are Gilbert and Sullivan played out?

Joe (*off*) Is there any truth in the rumour that Richard D'Oyly Carte is about to launch a competition to find Gilbert and Sullivan a script?

Geraldine (*off*) What is happening at the Savoy?

Jessie (*off*) Is D'Oyly Carte's Empire about to collapse?

Carte (*rising and pacing between Gilbert at his desk and Sullivan on the podium*) Arthur, things are getting desperate. You must have heard what people are saying. We must have a new piece.

Sullivan I am not writing for a lozenge!

Carte Is that all that is holding us up?

Sullivan I am not writing for a lozenge!

Carte Gilbert has told me he has provided you with a plot and you refuse to work on it.

Sullivan Yes, but it is the same old plot he keeps trying to fob off on me.

Carte Surely it will do?

Sullivan Look, Carte, if he will find another subject, I—I will write the music. But I am not writing for a lozenge.

Gilbert The time has come when I must state with great reluctance that I cannot construct another plot for your next opera.

Sullivan Further discussion is useless. I regret it very much.

Carte Gilbert, I'll sue you for every penny I can get out of you.

Gilbert Damn and blast you, Carte. Don't come threatening me. Sue me? I'll sue you for malicious behaviour. It is Sullivan you ought to shout at, he turns all my ideas down.

Carte (*punctured*) I know, I know . . .

Gilbert Don't keep saying "I know, I know" all the time, it is exceedingly tedious.

Carte But, Gilbert, old man, you must have other ideas.

Gilbert I have not another blasted idea in my head.

Carte Look, I hate to remind you of your contract . . .

Gilbert (*rising and taking a Japanese sword from his umbrella stand in mistake for his walking-stick*) Damn, damn you, I've given him a plot!

Sullivan I'm not writing for a lozenge!
Gilbert Now look here, Sullivan . . .

Gilbert, still waving the sword, comes running towards the podium. Sullivan rises and runs away. Carte tries to calm them and then exits

Piano—"The Mikado". Gilbert looks at the sword: inspiration dawns!

Sullivan! Sullivan! No, no, come back, don't go away, now . . .
Sullivan (*shouting*) Get away, you madman!
Gilbert (*continuing to chase Sullivan round and round the podium*) Stand still, no more lozenges—it'll have a Japanese setting. Call it *The Mikado* —or *The Town of Titipu*. We'll have a joke at all the japanning that's going on . . .

Sullivan stops, exhausted

We'll go to the Japanese village in Knightsbridge and find someone, Japanese, to coach the actors in deportment.

Gilbert begins to mince around: watched by a frightened and astonished Sullivan

Miya Suma, miya Suma.
Sullivan Er—quite.

Gilbert advances on Sullivan, who—still not convinced that Gilbert is all right—backs away a little

Gilbert Costumes colourful, especially made of pure silk—at Liberty's in Regent Street. But the principals' costumes we'll get from Japan, the real thing—ancient . . . Samurai. We'll have armour . . .
Sullivan The Japanese are rather small—on the whole—that's only a point—not a criticism. Armour might not fit . . .
Gilbert All right, scrap the armour. We don't need armour. But it all appeals to you . . .?
Sullivan Why not? Why not . . .?

The Company come on for "The Mikado" sequence carrying fans

THE MIKADO   **15**
(con
All Behold the Lord High Executioner!
    A personage of noble rank and title—
    A dignified and potent officer,
        Whose functions are particularly vital!
        Defer, defer,
    To the Lord High Executioner! Defer, defer,
    To the Noble Lord
    To the Lord High Executioner!

TIT WILLOW

Ko-Ko (Sullivan) On a tree by a river, a little tom tit,
Sang willow, tit-willow, tit-willow.
And I said to him, dickey bird
Why do you sit? Singing willow, tit-willow, tit-willow?
Is it weakness of intellect, birdy, I cried,
Or a rather tough worm in your little inside?
With a shake of his poor little head
He replied . . . Oh . . .

THREE LITTLE MAIDS

Girls Three little maids from school are we,
Pert as a schoolgirl well can be,
Filled to the brim with girlish glee,
Three little maids from school!
Yum-Yum (Sybil) Everything is a source of fun. (*Chuckle*)
Peep-Bo (Jessie) Nobody's safe, for we care for none! (*Chuckle*)
Pitti-Sing (Geraldine) Life is a joke that's just begun! (*Chuckle*)
All Three little maids from school!
  (*Dancing*)
Three little maids who, all unwary,
Come from a ladies' seminary,
Freed from its genius tutelary—
(*Suddenly demure*)
Three little maids from school!

A WANDERING MINSTREL I

Nankipoo (Joe) A wandering minstrel I—
A thing of shreds and patches,
of ballads, songs and snatches,
And dreamy lullaby!

HERE'S A HOWDEDO!

Yum-Yum (Jessie) Here's a howdedo. If I marry you
When your time has come to perish
Then the maiden whom you cherish
(Must be slaughtered too!)
(*Repeat* "*Here's a howdedo*"—*twice*)
Ko-Ko (Grossmith) Here's a pretty mess. In a month or less
I must die without a wedding
Let the bitter tears I'm shedding,
Witness my distress.
(Here's a pretty mess) (*Repeat twice*)
(Here's a state of things!) (*Repeat twice*)

Ko-Ko (Sullivan) Here's a state of thing. To her life she clings
    Matrimonial devotion doesn't seem to suit her notion
    Burial it brings!

THE MOON AND I

Katishy (Sybil) Ah! Pray make no mistake
    We are not shy
    We're very wide awake
    The moon and I.
    (*Repeat the last two lines*)

FOR HE'S GOING TO MARRY YUM-YUM

Carte For he's going to marry Yum-Yum, Yum-Yum,
    Your anger pray bury
    For all will be merry
    I think you had better succumb,
    And join our expressions of glee.
Grossmith On this subject I pray you be dumb, dumb, dumb,
    You'll find there are many who'd wed for a penny
    The word for your guidance is mum, mum, mum
    There's lots of good fish in the sea.
Chorus On the subject we pray you be dumb, dumb, dumb,
    We think you had better succumb, cumb, cumb,
    You'll find.

Scream

MY OBJECT ALL SUBLIME

Mikado (Gilbert) The advertising quack who wearies
    With tales of countless cures,
        His teeth, I've enacted,
        Shall all be extracted
    By terrified amateurs.
The music-hall singer attends a series
    Of masses and fugues and "ops"
        By Bach, interwoven
        With Spohr and Beethoven,
    At classical Monday Pops.

The billiard sharp whom anyone catches,
    His doom's extremely hard—
    He's made to dwell—
    In a dungeon cell
    On a spot that's always barred.
And there he plays extravagant matches
    In fitless finger-stalls
        On a cloth untrue,
        With a twisted cue

And elliptical billiard balls! HA! HA!
My object all sublime
I shall achieve in time—
To let the punishment fit the crime—
The punishment fit the crime;
And make each prisoner pent
Unwillingly represent
A source of innocent merriment!
Of innocent merriment!

THE FLOWERS THAT BLOOM IN THE SPRING

Grossmith The flowers that bloom in the spring,
Tra la,
Breathe promise of merry sunshine—
As we merrily dance and we sing,
Tra la,
We welcome the hope that they bring,
Tra la,
Of a summer of roses and wine.
And that's what we mean when we say that a thing
Is welcome as flowers that bloom in the spring.
Tra la la la la la, etc.
The flowers that bloom in the spring.
All Tra la la la, etc. (*Refer to score*)

DERRY DOWN

All If that is so, sing derry down derry
It's evident very our tastes are one
Away we'll go and merrily marry
Nor tardily tarry till day is done. (*Repeat*)

Sing derry down derry,
We'll merrily marry
Nor tardily tarry
'Til day is done.

All exit except Carte and Gilbert, who go to their places. Joe returns with a newspaper which he gives to Carte

Joe Twentieth October, eighteen eighty-six. With *The Mikado* a success all over the world. Some people enjoy reading their morning papers. Mr Carte! . . . (*He goes to Gilbert and gives him a paper*) Others do not!

Joe exits

Gilbert Carte. (*He goes to Carte*)

Carte Ah, Gilbert. I see *The Mikado* has broken all records in New York.

Gilbert Where's the music for *Ruddigore*? I've been trying to pin him down for weeks. He's never in. Every time I open a newspaper, what do I find? "Sir Arthur Sullivan attends Royal Garden Party." "Sir Arthur Sullivan at Ascot." "Sir Arthur Sullivan at Henley." "Sir Arthur Sullivan with Mrs Ronalds." So much for all the work he is supposed to be doing. (*He returns to his desk*)

Carte Well, he must have done some, because I hear his new oratorio opens at Leeds tonight.

Piano starts

Oratorio: "The Golden Legend"   16

> *Jessie, Sybil, Geraldine and Grossmith enter with newspapers*

Jessie *Leeds Mercury.* How can we describe the scene which followed *The Golden Legend*'s first performance—the audience rose to its feet in thundering approval. Never was there a more heartfelt ovation.

Sybil *Daily Telegraph.* A greater, more undoubted triumph has never been within my experience.

Geraldine *Musical World.* Hitherto it has been difficult to place the composer of *Pirates of Penzance*, but now his fame rests on a different basis.

Grossmith *The World.* Sullivan is the Mozart of England.

The "Newspapers" exit. Sullivan enters and goes to the podium

Gilbert hits his desk

Gilbert Where is the music for *Ruddigore*?

Sullivan (*on his telephone*) Sorry, Bertie, another interruption. . . . Yes, of course you shall have the Jubilee Ode by the end of the month. I've been so busy with my oratorio. . . . She said what? . . . Oh, how very kind. . . . Yes of course, *her* will is my . . . Yes. Good-bye. (*He replaces the receiver. To Carte*) The Queen has just asked me to write a grand opera, she said I'd do it so well . . .

Carte and Gilbert rise and go to Sullivan

Gilbert Where's the music for *Ruddigore* . . .?

Sullivan What?

Gilbert Where is it?

Carte (*apologetically*) Arthur, we hope to go into rehearsals next week. May we see some of it?

Sullivan Umm.

Gilbert Please?

Sullivan Well, umm.

An awkward silence

Gilbert You haven't even started on it, have you?

Carte It's too bad, Arthur . . .

Gilbert Too bad. You had a commitment to us and you spend your time flying your kite. We are supposed to open in a matter of weeks.

Sullivan But I've been very busy . . .

Gilbert And made yourself ill into the bargain. You look like death warmed up. Damn you, Sullivan. We must cash in on *The Mikado*'s success. Tell him, Carte.

Carte (*having weighed up the situation*) Arthur, I'm very disappointed in you.

Gilbert Disappointed!

Carte We'll have to postpone *Ruddigore*, but please hurry.

Gilbert For God's sake, Sullivan, hurry.

Carte and Gilbert exit

Sullivan How do you expect me to get through all this work, all of you? Aren't I to be allowed a life of my own? In the space of a year I have to write a comic opera, a hymn tune and an oratorio. What do you think I am? A barrel-organ—you turn the handle and I churn out the music to order? Well, you shall have your comic opera—but I warn you— things are going to change. I will not be dictated to. I will not. I will not . . .

RUDDIGORE   17

Carte enters as Sir Roderick

Sir Roderick (Carte) Beware! Beware! Beware!

Rob (Sullivan) Gaunt vision, who art thou
    That thus, with icy glare
    And stern relentless brow,
    Appearest, who knows how?

Sir Roderick I am the spectre of the late
    Sir Roderick Murgatroyd
    Who comes to warn thee that thy fate
    Thou canst not now avoid.

Rob Alas, poor ghost!

Sir Roderick The pity you express for nothing goes
    We spectres are a jollier crew
    Than you perhaps suppose!
    Ha! Ha! Ha! Ha!

THE GHOST'S HIGH NOON

When the night wind howls in the chimney cowls, and the
    bat in the moonlight flies,
And inky clouds, like funeral shrouds, sail over the
    midnight skies—
When the footpads quail at the night-bird's wail, and
    black dogs bay at the moon,

Then is the spectres' holiday—then is the ghosts' high noon!
For then is the ghosts' high noon
High noon
Then is the ghosts' high noon.
As the sob of the breeze sweeps over the trees, and the
    mists lie low on the fen,
From grey tomb-stones are gathered the bones that once
    were women and men,
And away they go, with a mop and a mow, to the revel
    that ends too soon,
For cockcrow limits our holiday—the dead of the night's
    high noon!
The dead of the night's high noon
High noon
The dead of the night's high noon.

Rob I recognize you now—you are the picture that hangs at the end of the gallery.

Sir Roderick In a bad light I am.

Rob Are you considered a good likeness?

Sir Roderick Pretty well. Flattering.

Rob Because as a work of art you are poor.

Sir Roderick I am crude in colour, because I have only been painted for ten years. In two centuries' time I shall be regarded as an old master and you will be very sorry you spoke so slightingly of me.

Rob And why, may I ask, have you left your frame?

Sir Roderick I have come to remind you that you are evading the conditions under which you are permitted to exist.

The Lights fade. Joe removes Carte's "Sir Roderick" cloak. The Lights come up to reveal Sullivan facing Gilbert and Carte

Sullivan What?

Carte I said that *Ruddigore* will not run. People have been booing and hissing—crying out "Bring back *The Mikado*". It will not run!

Sullivan Well excuse me, are you blaming me?

Gilbert Yes. If you'd got down to your work earlier instead of flying your kite, and if you had written music less suited to a cathedral, and more suited to comic opera, the audiences might have enjoyed it more . . .

Sullivan Strange that the music should be under attack—there was so little opportunity for music in *Ruddigore*, people wondered what I had to do with it. It was just a straight play with a few songs thrown in . . .

Gilbert And half of those should have been cut.

Carte Gentlemen, gentlemen, this never gets us anywhere.

Gilbert If he'd put more effort into it instead of flying his kite . . .

Carte Lots of things wrong with it. *Your* title for a start . . . *Ruddigore*—people found it offensive.

Gilbert What should I have called it? "Kensington Gore?" Or "Not Half So Good As *The Mikado*"? How about that, eh? Or—"Forgive The Music, The Composer Is Only Half With Us"! That's a good one . . .

Sullivan I'm not going to stay here listening to this. I have a boat train to catch. (*He goes to his podium and sits*)

Gilbert See what I mean? His work means nothing to him. We are a mere intrusion on his holidays.

Carte Go easy on him, Gilbert. He's probably hurt, it's not a happy situation for any of us having a failure on our hands . . .

Gilbert I don't know what this fuss is about. *Ruddigore*, a failure? It will net me around seven thousand pounds. I could wish for a few more failures like that . . .

Carte Yes, but it is still a come down after *The Mikado*. In this business you are only as good as your latest offering. We shall have to think very carefully about the next one.

Gilbert What does the public want?

Joe enters with a copy of "The Times" for Carte

Carte Look, we must think upon new lines. *The Mikado* succeeded be cause it was fresh, it startled people . . . We must think that way again. There was an article in *The Times* the other day. Did you see it? (*To Joe*). Thank you (*He takes the newspaper. Reading*) "A real comic opera dealing with neither topsy-turveydom nor fairies would be a great novelty and a more splendid success than anything we are likely to see during the present dramatic season . . ." Why not think on those lines, Gilbert? A good strong plot would keep Sullivan up to the mark, and he does need keeping up to the mark, I agree—and it may also go some way towards satisfying his grand opera—pretensions—just this once . . .

Gilbert But it wouldn't be comic opera, would it?

Carte I'm sure a writer of your talent and experience could write comedy, in such a way that it does not immediately appear like comedy. With some philosophy! Well, after all, there must be some statement *you'd* like to make that would last . . .

Gilbert Sugar the pill, you mean?

Carte Yes.

Gilbert All right. Just to show that I am not quite the barbaric buffoon I have been called at times, I'll try to do as you have asked. But I rely on you to keep Sullivan up to the mark. (*He sits at his desk*)

Carte You leave Sullivan to me.

Carte walks over to Sullivan's podium

Well, Arthur, what do you think of it?

Sullivan I think we've finally won, Richard.

Carte I'm glad. I did talk very seriously to him.

Sullivan This new plot of his is very good, very—human. No topsy-turveydom. Historical setting. Tower of London. He got the idea from a poster on the underground railway. I can hardly believe it.

Carte Yes, and this may help to pave the way for something of a more serious nature.

Sullivan A real opera—on a big scale?

Carte I cannot say more than this at the moment, Arthur, but my new theatre is coming along, it's coming along. It will house only opera— The English Royal Opera Company. I need hardly say, I am expecting a great deal from Sir Arthur Sullivan.

Sullivan Thank you, Richard . . .

Carte So do this one with Gilbert, eh? Just to pave the way . . .

Sullivan Yes, all right. (*He goes to the podium*) Where is he now?

Carte Up on Tower Green I should imagine. As you say—I think we've won. (*He goes to his table*)

The Company enter

Gilbert (*writing*) When a jester
    Is outwitted
    Feelings fester
    Heart is lead
    Food for fishes
    Only fitted
    Jester wishes
    He was dead.

Sullivan (*suddenly rising*) Mr Gilbert! This is a music rehearsal.

Gilbert (*rising*) I am aware of that, sir!

Sullivan And I am in charge of it.

Gilbert You, sir, are in charge of the crotchets, minims and quavers and all those other absurd characters. *I* am in charge of the *words*—the action—and everything else . . .

Sullivan But you have no right to be here today, sir.

Gilbert I've as much right as you, sir.

Sullivan Only with *my* permission! Music rehearsal days are *my* days.

Carte (*rising and moving to them*) Yes, come on, Gilbert, old man, settle down.

Gilbert You keep out of it and do your sums—money is your game, Carte! Confine your thoughts to money.

Carte How dare you!

Sullivan Oh, this is impossible. Get me my coat!

Gilbert Stay here and earn *your* money.

Sullivan You—you—don't need me! You don't need a musician. What you need is a barrel-organ . . .

Gilbert Yes—I've already got the monkey!

Sullivan What did you say, sir?

Carte I give up! (*He goes to his table*)

Sullivan (*pointing across Carte at Gilbert*) Let me tell you, sir. I am entitled to some respect from *you*!

Gilbert I'll give you respect when you behave worthily of respect.

Joe whistles. The Lights change. Gilbert, Sullivan and Carte freeze

Joe In two days' time Sir Arthur will finally bring himself to speak to Mr Gilbert.

Gilbert These shocks and disturbances are far too much for me, let's have no more of them. I'm too old . . .

Sullivan Nonsense . . .

Gilbert I am, I am a ruin—you should see me—by moonlight. Put a twig of ivy in my hair and an owl under my arm and Tintern Abbey's got nothing on me.

Sullivan Gilbert, I have to confess that there is one song that has beaten me—I'm sorry but I just cannot set it.

Gilbert If you can't set it, cut it.

Sullivan But the words are so good. We can't lose it.

Gilbert Which one is it?

Sullivan The one with the "Heighdy" chorus.

Gilbert Oh, that's a bugger, that one.

Sullivan Look, I know I always ask you to keep your ideas for tunes to yourself, but this time do you think you could give me a clue?

Gilbert I'll tell you where I got the idea from. It is something I've heard sailors singing down in Cornwall, when I've been on my yacht. I think it is an old carol—it goes something like this.

The piano starts   **18**

THE YEOMEN OF THE GUARD

THE YEOMAN SONG

Gilbert I have a song to sing, O!

Elsie (Sybil) What is your song, O?

Point (Sullivan) It is sung to the moon
      By a love-lorn loon,
    Who fled from the mocking throng, O!
  It's the song of a merryman, moping mum,
  Whose soul was sad, and whose glance was glum,
  Who sipped no sup, and who craved no crumb,
    As he sighed for the love of a ladye!

All   Heighdy! Heighdy!
      Misery me, lackadaydee!
  He sipped no sup, and he craved no crumb,
    As he sighed for the love of a ladye!

Elsie (Sybil) I have a song to sing, O!

Point What is your song, O?

Elsie   It is sung with the ring
      Of the songs maids sing
  Who love with a love life-long, O!
  It's the song of a merry maid, nestling near,
  Who loved her lord—and who dropped a tear
  At the moan of the merryman, moping mum,
  Whose soul was sad, and whose glance was glum,
  Who sipped no sup, and who craved no crumb,
    As he sighed for the love of a ladye!

All   Heighdy! Heighdy!
           Misery me, lackadaydee!
        He sipped no sup, and he craved no crumb,
           As he sighed for the love of a ladye.

All but Gilbert, Sullivan and Carte exit

Sullivan hands Carte a letter then sits on the podium

Gilbert A what?

Carte A cipher.

Gilbert Give it to me. (*Reading*) "Except during vocal rehearsals and the two orchestral rehearsals, I am a cipher in the theatre. They are Gilbert's pieces with music added by me. Unless a change is made I should wish to give it up altogether." Of all the confounded . . . (*He paces*)

Carte Calm down, Gilbert. Calm down.

Gilbert You know who is at the back of all this, don't you?

Carte I know, I know . . .

Gilbert Queen Victoria. And you've made matters worse with your meddling . . .

Carte Me?

Gilbert Yes, you. You with all your plans to open your new opera house next spring—with his opera. Opera . . . I go on record now as saying that the whole thing will be a gigantic flop. You might as well open a museum . . .

Carte Time will tell.

Gilbert Yes it will. Where is Sullivan? Riviera, I suppose. Leaving me to cope with all the real work here. And he says *he*'s the cipher in the theatre. What, pray, am I? The bloody doormat. Doesn't he realize that I have sacrificed my ambition to write these operas? I am a serious dramatist. Why must it always be Sullivan who has sacrificed himself?

Sullivan I find comic opera distasteful. It no longer suits me.

Gilbert All right. All right. Do both.

Sullivan No, I've been a slave to comic opera too long. I do not want to spend any more of my life clothing stock figures in music. It's all such a chore.

Gilbert Well, I'm certainly not having my plot, my words drowned in music. Comic opera is bad enough. It's still all Sullivan . . .

Sullivan I have spent the last twelve years of my life sacrificing my music to your words . . .

Gilbert Sacrifice. Sacrifice. Have I not sacrificed myself for you? Very well, I am sorry if you've been forced to efface yourself in our association. If you have actually suffered in silence for twelve years, you have nobody to blame but yourself. If we ever meet again, let it not be as master and servant but as master and master . . .

Carte (*as Don Alhambra*) As the country is in a state of insurrection, it is absolutely necessary that you assume the reins of government at once: and until it is decided which of you shall be king, I have arranged that

you will reign jointly, so that no question shall arise hereafter as to the
validity of any of your acts.

Sullivan As one individual?

Carte As one individual?

Gilbert Like this?

Carte Well, something like that.

The Company enter for "The Gondoliers"   **19**

THE GONDOLIERS

Antonio (Grossmith) For the merriest fellows are we, tra la
　　(*See score for "tralas"*)
　　　That ply on the emerald sea, tra la;

Chorus With loving and laughing,
　　　　And quipping and quaffing,
　　　We're happy as happy can be, tra la—
　　　　As happy as happy can be!
　　(*Many "tralas", see score for "tralas"*)

Tessa (Sybil) When a merry maiden marries,
　　　Sorrow goes and pleasure tarries;
　　　　Every sound becomes a song,
　　　　All is right, and nothing's wrong!
　　　From today and ever after
　　　Let our tears be tears of laughter.
　　　　Every sigh that finds a vent
　　　　Be a sigh of sweet content!

*The Company exits after "The Gondoliers", except Gilbert and Sullivan.
They sit, possibly on a skip. Sullivan begins to sing "Take a pair of
sparkling eyes". Joe enters and stands behind Gilbert and Sullivan. Gilbert
and Sullivan sit, looking worn-out, and speak their lines out front*

TAKE A PAIR OF SPARKLING EYES

Marco (Sullivan) Take a pair of sparkling eyes,
　　　Hidden, ever and anon,
　　　　In a merciful eclipse—
　　Do not heed their mild surprise—
　　　Having passed the Rubicon,
　　　　Take a pair of rosy lips;
　　Take a figure trimly planned—
　　　Such as admiration whets
　　　　(Be particular in this);
　　Take a tender little hand,
　　　Fringed with dainty fingerettes,
　　Press it, Press it—in parenthesis;—
　　Ah! Take all these, you lucky man—
　　Take and keep them, if you can! (*Etc.*)

Joe And after a very successful opening of *The Gondoliers* Mr Gilbert will write to Sir Arthur Sullivan . . .

Gilbert "I must thank you again for the magnificent work you have put into the piece. It gives one a chance of shining right through into the twentieth century with reflected light."

Joe And Sir Arthur Sullivan will reply to Mr Gilbert.

Sullivan "Don't talk of reflected light. In such a perfect book as *The Gondoliers* you shine with an individual brilliancy which no other writer can hope to attain. If any thanks are due anywhere, they should be from me to you."

Gilbert Take a pretty little cot—
    Quite a miniature affair—
        Hung about with trellised vine,
    Furnish it upon the spot
      With the treasures rich and rare
      I've endeavoured to define.
    Live to love and love to live—
      You will ripen at your ease,
        Growing on the sunny side—
    Fate has nothing more to give.
      You're a dainty man to please
      If you are not satisfied.
    Ah! Take my counsel, happy man;
    Act upon it, if you can!

Carte enters with a ledger. He hands it to Joe, who takes it to Gilbert, open

Carpets?

THE CARPET QUARREL

Carte Don't raise your voice to me, Gilbert.

Gilbert Five hundred pounds for bloody carpets?

Carte And don't swear.

Gilbert Just explain these accounts.

Carte They are preliminary expenses for *The Gondoliers*.

Gilbert I don't see where carpets come into it.

Carte Just look what you spent on set and costumes. And I never complained. You never consulted me.

Gilbert That's beside the point. I don't expect to be stung for bills which have nothing to do with me. Like five hundred pounds for front of house carpets.

Carte If you look carefully, you'll see it's not five hundred but one hundred and forty.

Gilbert Damn you, Carte, I'm not paying a penny for carpets. They have nothing to do with me . . .

Carte You rent this theatre. Our contract states that you share costs in maintaining repairs . . .

Gilbert The public come to see my plays, not to gawp at carpets illuminated by electric lamps.

Carte I've done everything I can for you. I've lied and told tales, raised money in the early days, everything. I found the best theatre I could—I did the best I could for it. I should just have put sawdust and spitoons down—and left you to it . . .

Gilbert I demand a new agreement.

Carte All right. I'LL raise your rent from four thousand to five thousand pounds.

Gilbert Then you can find yourself another author.

Carte Very well, that is understood. You will write no more for the Savoy.

Gilbert I made you, Carte. You build up your empire, and you'd kick away the ladder by which you climbed.

Carte (*sitting at his table*) Get out of my office.

Gilbert goes to Sullivan

Gilbert Five hundred pounds for carpets. We'll fight him together.

Sullivan Please, Gilbert, I am ill—I don't want to fight anybody. I want to be left alone to work in peace.

Gilbert You cannot be left in peace while Carte builds his empire at our expense.

Sullivan I don't see the point of destroying everything we've done for a carpet worth a hundred and forty pounds.

Gilbert (*to Carte*) I shall take you to court, sir. ·

Carte Do so.

Sullivan (*rising*) Please, please, I beg you, no more of this. The whole wretched business is making me ill. I can't work. We are making laughing stocks of ourselves. And the Company is going to pieces.

Gilbert There is a principle at stake here, Sullivan. This man is nothing but a bloody capitalist.

Carte (*rising*) It amazes me, Gilbert, that you can throw that word at me with impunity. You are a born capitalist. How much money have you made in the last few years?

Gilbert I've earned it.

Carte And you've used others to earn it for you which makes you a capitalist like me. It's always amused me, Gilbert, how in your plays, you've come out against the money-makers, you've supported the poor and down-trodden—and yet you've used everybody for your own ends. And you wouldn't even pay a member of your own company anything like what he is worth. This house of yours at Grim's Dyke. How many servants will it employ there? Forty or more, I'm told.

Gilbert How many servants do you have? How much money have you made?

Carte You, sir, we are talking about you.

Gilbert I want to talk about you.

Sullivan Stop it, both of you.

Gilbert You, sir, are an exploiter. You have exploited me, and you have exploited him.

Carte Have I exploited you, Arthur?

Sullivan No.

Gilbert I see. Yes, I see. Carte, I give you notice that you will not perform any libretti of mine after Christmas eighteen ninety. In fact, after the withdrawal of *The Gondoliers* the combined work of Gilbert and Sullivan will be heard no more.

Carte So be it.

The Company enter

FINALE

A Stage Hand winds the watch. The remaining actors and actresses speak out the following: taking each line in turn

Joe And all *for one hundred and forty pounds*!   20

The piano starts

Jessie Gilbert will take Carte to court—and put in an Official Receiver to check the account.

Grossmith There will be two more Savoy operas. Both will fail.

Joe Both will write with other collaborators—both will have less success.

Jessie Gilbert will eventually stage his "Lozenge Play"—it will have two hundred and twenty-nine performances.

Sybil Sullivan will realize his dream—his opera *Ivanhoe*—at Carte's new Opera House . . .

Geraldine But it will play only one hundred and forty performances.

Sybil Queen Victoria, after suggesting that Sullivan should write an opera, will not actually go to see it.

Geraldine But she will call for a private performance of *The Gondoliers* at Windsor Castle.

Joe And the Royal Opera House, Carte's great ambition—will become the Palace Theatre—the home of—musical comedy.

Jessie Gilbert's gout will get worse.

Geraldine Sullivan's kidney disease will make him weaker.

Joe After the Twenty-first Birthday performance of *The Sorcerer* they will enter from different sides of the stage, bow to the audience, speak not a word to each other: leave the theatre separately and never see each other again.

Sybil Twenty-second November nineteen hundred: finally beaten by the kidney disease that has wrecked his life, Sullivan will die.

Sullivan exits

Geraldine Mrs Ronalds will be just too late to be with him in his final moment.

Sybil On Queen Victoria's Order he will be buried in St Paul's.

Jessie As the procession passes along the Embankment, D'Oyly Carte will drag himself from his sick bed to the window to see the last of his old friend. And he will have to be carried back to bed.

Joe Where four months later, he will die.

Carte exits

Jessie Gilbert will live on into the twentieth century.
Grossmith He will become notorious as a Justice of the Peace.
Jessie And an even more notorious motorist.
Grossmith And in nineteen hundred and seven, twenty-four years after Sullivan, he will be knighted.
Jessie Twenty-ninth May nineteen hundred and eleven, he will go to the rescue of two girls who are swimming in his lake. And he will drown.

Gilbert exits

Geraldine He always said he wished to die on a summer's day in his own garden.
Jessie He will leave over a hundred thousand pounds.

Jessie exits

Sybil Sullivan will leave less than fifty thousand pounds.

Sybil and Geraldine exit

Joe D'Oyly Carte will leave more than two hundred thousand pounds.
Grossmith Throughout the twentieth century the operas will sweep the world—playing in every opera house and in every town—and their tunes will be the best-known tunes—and their immortality will lie on the lips of the man who whistles them in the street.

Grossmith exits

Joe sweeps the stage and whistles music as he does so. The Lights slowly fade

Gilbert (*off*) I must thank you again for the magnificent work you have put into the piece. It gives one a chance of shining right through into the twentieth century with reflected light.
Sullivan (*off*) Don't talk of reflected light. In such a perfect book as *The Gondoliers* you shine with an individual brilliancy which no other writer can hope to attain. If any thanks are due anywhere, they should be from me to you.

CURTAIN

FURNITURE AND PROPERTY LIST

ACT I

On stage: **Gilbert:**
High desk. *On it:* writing materials, scripts
High backed stool
Umbrella stand with walking-stick
Hat stand
Screen
Sullivan:
Podium
Music stand, music and baton
Padded seat
Table. *On it:* sheets of music, scores, scripts
Hat stand
Screen
Carte:
Table. *On it:* writing materials, documents, contracts, scripts
Upright armchair
2 small chairs
Hat stand

Piano, stool and music (on stage or in auditorium)

Off stage: Broom **(Joe)**
               Music sheet **(Grossmith)**
               Music sheets and scores **(The Company)**
               Courtroom unit for *Trial by Jury*, with books and papers on Bench
                  (set by **Stage hands**)
               Tray of filled champagne glasses **(Joe)**
               Card table with "Bombay" pictures, including black one **(Joe)**
               Placards **(Stage hands)**
               Luggage—suitcases **(Stage hands)**

Personal: **Joe:** watch

ACT II

Set: Telephone on **Gilbert's** table
               Telephone on **Carte's** table
               Telephone on **Sullivan's** table
               Pad and pencil on **Carte's** table
               New libretto on **Gilbert's** table
               Japanese sword in **Gilbert's** umbrella stand

Off stage: Light bulb on cushion, hammer **(Joe)**
               Opened letter **(Sullivan)**
               Tray of filled champagne glasses **(Joe)**
               Note on salver **(Joe)**
               Sword **(Stage hand)**
               Letter **(Geraldine)**
               Fans **(The Company,** for *Mikado* sequence)
               Newspaper **(Joe)**
               4 newspapers **(Jessie, Sybil, Geraldine, Grossmith)**
               Copy of *The Times* **(Joe)**
               Letter **(Sullivan)**
               Ledger **(Carte)**

LIGHTING PLOT

NOTE: The following is a basic plot only. Spot cues for songs, etc may be added as facilities allow

Property fittings required: nil
Composite setting on bare stage

ACT I

To open:	Overall general lighting	
Cue 1	**Sybil:** "To my hesitating heart." *Fade to Black-out*	(Page 29)
Cue 2	Cheers from the **Company** *Return to full lighting*	(Page 29)

ACT II

To open:	As Act I opening	
Cue 3	**Gilbert:** ". . . on my *new* telephone." *Golden spot up on* **Sullivan**	(Page 39)
Cue 4	**Carte:** "Splendid." *Fade golden spot*	(Page 40)
Cue 5	**Sir Roderick:** ". . . are permitted to exist." *Fade to Black-out: fade up again when* **Sullivan, Carte** *and* **Gilbert** *are in position*	(Page 56)
Cue 6	**Gilbert:** ". . . behave worthily of respect." *Lighting change to cover prelude to "Yeomen" excerpt*	(Page 58)
Cue 7	**Joe** starts to sweep stage *Slow fade to Curtain*	(Page 65)